Bill Rodel
P.O. Box 2012
Lewiston, Id.
83501

BIRDHUNTER

Herb "Booth"

BIRDHUNTER

A celebration of wild birds,

fine guns, and staunch dogs

by Richard S. Grozik

Safari Press Inc.

P.O. Box 3095, Long Beach, California 90803

Grozik, R.

Second edition

Safari Press Inc.

1997, Long Beach, California

ISBN 1-57157-061-6

Library of Congress Catalog Card Number: 96-71773

10 9 8 7 6 5 4 3 2

Readers wishing to receive the Safari Press catalog, featuring many fine books on big-game hunting, wingshooting, and sporting firearms, should write to Safari Press Inc., P.O. Box 3095, Long Beach, CA 90803, USA. Tel: (714) 894-9080, or visit our Web site at www.safaripress.com.

Contents

Acknowledgments vi
Introduction vii
Foreword x
Dedication xiii

Birth of a Birdhunter 1

Broomstraw 7

Sixteen Ounces 17

Birds of a Feather 29

Luck of the Irish 37

Fit to Shoot 45

Will-O'-the-Wisp 57

All-American Game Gun 65

Grouse Country 79

Smitty 87

Best Bird Guns 95

Gray Ghosts 103

Graven Images 111

Driven Birds 119

Ahead of the Game 127

Just One More Gun 133

Stock and Trade 141

The Gathering Place 145

Acknowledgments

Nothing of value lingers unless it is held in the hearts and souls of those who have an abiding reverence for life. This book would not have been written were it not for many such individuals who shared their hearts and souls with me—Uncle John Gualdoni, Uncle Steve Grozik, Frank Compa, Mark Magden, Wilbert Williams, Art Lefeurve and Bingo, Baron McDuff and Duffy II. All are gone now but alive on the pages of this book and in my heart.

To my lovely wife, Colette, who has endured without complaint the trials and privations of my lifelong quest, with gun and quill, for adventure afield. And to my hunting companions, four-legged and two, who trek over hill and dale with me in search of lasting significance for this life we have been given, I wish you God's speed, abundant game, and a heart full of lingering memories.

Portions of what is written in this book have appeared in different form and title in the following publications: *Ducks Unlimited, Shooting Sportsman, RGS Drummer, Double Gun Journal, Quail Unlimited, and Fur, Fish & Game.*

All of what is written herein is hopefully, in some small way, a tribute to all those kindred souls, past and present, whose reverence for the sporting life has enriched us all.

Introduction

Few things in life are as sacred to me as a well-balanced game gun, a biddable bird dog, and an understanding spouse. I have been blessed, at one time or another, with all three. Only true friendship can come close to the profound satisfaction I get from keeping gun, dog, and wife in balance with the seasons. However, I know that if I do not religiously maintain this holy alliance, all hell can break loose, usually on or around opening day.

My first conquest in this eternal sporting triangle has proven to be one of the most rewarding experiences in my wingshooting rite of passage. Selecting the perfect game gun, like marrying the ideal mate, has renewed my faith in miracles. My perennial quest to possess that poetic blend of flaming English walnut and tempered ordnance steel has introduced me to a colorful cast of characters, many of whom have become cherished friends and lifelong hunting companions. Perhaps when I finally wrest this elusive wonder gun from the hands of fate, my mental and emotional growth will resume its haphazard development.

Second only to my search for the perfect game gun is my desire to own just one more good bird dog—one that I can brag on and locate once it is free of the kennel. My impeccably pedigreed gun dog must possess trainable instincts that can at once discern the troublesome difference between fur, antlers, and quills. In addition to exhibiting blind obedience to its woefully untrained master, my purebred hunting companion must point stylishly, hold steady to wing and shot, and tenderly retrieve gamebirds while I fill its ears with empty threats and all manner of confusing commands. Given these simple parameters, I am convinced there is very little truth to the commonly held belief that I would be living an enchanted existence if I owned just one such bird dog in the course of my lifetime. To be perfectly honest, I'll never admit to owning any other kind of dog.

Unfortunately, my selection of an understanding spouse has proven a real disappointment—for her, not me. During our courtship, I promised her that my love affair with the fall woods, like her eagerness to learn how to clean and prepare wild game, would diminish over the years. Strangely enough, she has become a wild-game gourmet, and I spend a lot of time polishing excuses on why I bring less of it home. I must confess that I probably expended more effort and money researching the pedigrees of my gun dogs than I did exploring the parentage and temperament of my lifelong soul mate. Perhaps a *forgiving* wife is what I really had in mind all along.

If any of this strikes a familiar chord, then you have exercised good judgment in purchasing this book. You may not find the solution to all your birdhunting afflictions or affectations on these pages, but you can take solace in knowing there are others who share your sentiment, if not your predicament.

I'm certain that my darling wife, biologically immune to simple explanations, will never truly understand my obsession with the outdoors. Complicated as it must sound to her, I survive the seasons simply by uncasing my infallible bird gun and following my polished bird dog into forest and field in wanton pursuit of wild birds on the wing. With any kind of luck, and maybe a dash of divine intervention, my forgiving spouse will always have dinner waiting when I get home. Sounds perfectly simple to me.

Foreword

Early October in a long distance conversation with my oldest son, I asked about guests for opening weekend. In addition to the almost sacred and traditional list of friends, he said he had invited Rich Grozik.

"*The Game Gun* Rich Grozik?"

"That's the one. You'll like him. He thinks about hunting the way you do, and he is one of the nicest guys around."

Some of us, Rich included, were fortunate to grow up with hunting and its accompaniments as an integral part of life. It was usually a part of being home. This book puffs a little fresh air on those embers of memory. It brightens past experience that may have seemed mundane in the shadows of wishes for new guns, perfect dogs and game-filled coverts.

It's a given—the blending of guns, dogs, and game into the oneness of hunting. The total is diminished by the lack of appreciation for any of these. But the balance need never include snobbery or pretense which doesn't fit well in a down-to-earth life outdoors.

Of most importance among all other aspects of field sport is the hunter's concept of that noble experience. We hunt without apology, take what is offered, and do our best to restore what is taken. It can be no other way for very long.

That seems harsh until you watch the same field every day and see the delicate balance shift to offer a cover full of healthy plant and animal life; or a desolate parcel inhabited by a few rodents, insects, and an occasional disheartened predator. All depends on the whims of nature, or as is too often the case, mankind's chemicals, farm practices, or human determination to love it to death. Modern responsible hunting must always embrace a twinge of hope linked with concern about what will be next year.

Competition for access to good hunting, solitude, and wild game alarms us. We stand witness to urban sprawl, the yearning of populations to live close to nature and bring the city with them. Not to mention vehicles that go damn near anywhere. Most wild things can put up with only so much of it. As places are lost, opportunities for hunting diminish. Each good time becomes a prize that needs time to age, ferment and finally reach its peak; to be served over and over again as refreshment to those who read or listen. It is the rebirth of an experience exposed for the taking. This book refreshes its readers.

Shotguns are all made with room for opinions. Rich has used his share of the space. He discusses shooting from an inquisitive perspective that could help most of us. Years ago I bought a nice old 16-gauge double with 2½-inch chambers. I finally found the right cartridge and used the gun. I was amazed at how well it handled. Sometime later I read a piece that Rich wrote about 16-gauge guns using cartridges with one-ounce loads. It told me precisely why I liked the gun so much. I've been comfortable shooting it ever since. Little adjustments learned from someone who has worked it out can make a great difference in how a gun handles. Consider a few hints from Rich's personal tales about gunsmiths, dealers, friends, and a most tolerant and loving wife.

Our weekend hunt was about as good as it could have been. Rich carried the restocked Smith 16 featured in a chapter of this book. What a dandy gun! He shoots it well. We had never met but I felt that I knew and had high regard for Rich Grozik before he arrived at our place to hunt. That weekend showed my earlier estimations to be low of the mark. My son was right.

We became reacquainted through this book. I'm honored to have been asked to pass it on to you. It's a delightful collection, simmered, distilled and ready for eager consumption.

Dan Busse
Bird City, Kansas

Dedication

*To my dad, John Grozik, who bought me
my first duck call, took me hunting, and taught
me to respect the outdoors and myself . . . and
to all men who take young men hunting.*

Birth of a Birdhunter

Hands cupped around eyes and nose pressed against plate glass, I stared covetously at the elegant double gun displayed across waves of royal blue velvet in the front window of the co-op hardware store. Its smoothly tapered barrels, intricate scroll engraving, and marble-cake walnut stock oozed quality. Even at the tender age of eleven, I knew there was something special about the shotgun. Each day that spring, on my way to and from school, I stopped by the store window to gaze trance-like at the fancy 12-bore that had all the men in town talking. It was a first-class bird gun, all right, a luxury few in the small coal-mining community would ever see, let alone possess.

Raffle tickets for the gun were ten dollars each, more than I could ever think of earning in the two weeks left before the drawing. I was dead sure that if I could buy just one ticket, the pristine side-by-side would be mine. To no avail, I pestered my father unmercifully for the money. It was seldom that a boy living in those parts during those times would ever own anything with hanging tags, except perhaps a pair of bib overalls.

While admiring the gun one afternoon, I watched a swaggering, cigar-smoking gentleman pull a wad of green bills from his pocket and buy a fistful of raffle tickets from the store manager. My heart sank. As much as I coveted the gun, I certainly didn't want some city slicker to leave town with it. On his way out of the store, the man glanced at the double, patted me on the head, and said, "Nice gun, huh, sonny?" Then he reached in his pocket. "Son," he commanded, "I want you to hold on to these tickets for me. I'll be out of town for quite a while. The hardware man says he knows your daddy and that you are a trustworthy lad. Said you'd no doubt be at the drawing and wouldn't mind holding on to my tickets." Being called "sonny" was insult enough, but rubbing it in with the tickets was almost more than I could take. Before I could protest his confidence in me, he continued, "Son, if I win the gun, I promise there'll be something in it for you when I return." He slowly sank behind the wheel of his shiny black sedan parked at the curb, then yelled, "See ya, sonny!" out the window as he sped away.

There was a large crowd on hand the night of the big gun drawing that Memorial Day. Hunters from a three-county area converged on the small town to try their luck. With arms extended over his head, the hardware store man paraded the old double around the flatbed that was parked on the main street for the occasion. He solicited the large crowd one last time to buy tickets, then went on to explain that the money raised from the raffle would help build the health clinic the town so desperately needed. My anxiety was further piqued as he began describing the gun in excruciating detail. "This is an unfired BHE-grade Parker double, new as the day it was

2

made. It has been graciously donated to us by Widow Gray. This was the last gun old Doc Gray bought before his stroke. He never did get a chance to take it birdhunting. "This handsome gun," he rambled on, "has 28-inch barrels, improved cylinder/modified chokes, and double ivory beads on the rib. And just take a gander at that beautifully engraved skeleton butt. Now, I know a lot of you may not be too fond of the straight grip, single trigger, and beavertail fore-end, but that's how Doc liked all his bird guns, so I'm sure it's a gun any good wingshooter can get used to."

"Aw, come on, Ed!" someone in the crowd shouted. "Draw the damn ticket. My wife doesn't know I'm here, and she'll have my hide if I'm not home soon."

I had all but rubbed the ink off the raffle tickets I held fanlike in my perspiring hands. After some

additional fanfare, Widow Gray drew the ticket from the wire drum, and I closed my eyes as the winning number was announced. The next thing I knew my dad was pounding me on the back and yelling, "We've got the number here, we've got the number!" I stumbled dreamlike up to the drawing stand with hoots and hollers from the crowd echoing in my head.

It took me most of that hot, dry summer to come back down to earth and realize the gun wasn't mine. Inwardly, I desperately hoped the stranger who had given me the tickets would never return to claim his prize. Dove season was just a few weeks away, and with no gun of my own, the beautiful BHE tortured me every time I looked at it. During the summer I had consumed every detail of the shapely side-by-side, from its delicately scroll-engraved receiver and dazzling blend of case colors to every glowing swirl in its deeply figured Circassian walnut stock. But I was still denied the true joy that shooting such a fine gun could bring. Eventually the temptation became unbearable. Certain the stranger would never return for his gun, I almost had my father convinced to let me try it out when a long, black sedan pulled up in our front yard. The driver rolled a stubby cigar from one side of his mouth to the other and flashed a wide grin at me from behind the steering wheel. "Hiya, sonny!" he blurted. "Is your daddy home?" The thought of giving up the Parker made me sick to my stomach.

The portly stranger strode up to the front porch with an oil-tanned leg-o'-mutton case tucked under his arm. Locusts sang in the sycamores as we exchanged introductions and made small talk on the steps. He told us he was a traveling hardware salesman from a large city upstate. Dad invited him to stay for supper. In spite of his boisterous ways, he was a gracious man who seemed to know a lot about bird guns and bird dogs. He lavished praise on Parker Brothers' use of forged steel and meticulous hand craftsmanship. He went on to explain that the BHE's serial number indicated it was made in the early 1930s, about the time Remington bought out the Meriden, Connecticut, gunmaker.

Bird guns and birdhunting dominated our conversation most of that late-summer evening. Later, as we said our farewells on the porch, the man promised to take me on a first-class quail hunt before season's end. He even said he'd let me shoot the BHE. Motioning with his arm, he asked me to follow him out to his car. He opened the trunk, carefully placed his cased Parker to one side, then pulled out a long, slender box. "Go ahead and open it, sonny," he boomed, "it's for you." I eagerly opened the Winchester-imprinted box and slid out a gleaming Model 37 single-shot .410, hanging tags and all. "How do you like 'er?" he asked with a concerned tone. But before I could answer, he barged on, "Maybe it doesn't have all the fancy fixin's of the Parker, but it'll bring down birds if you point 'er right." He climbed into his car, said he'd be calling me soon, then rumbled off through the dust with a long wave good-bye. I never saw him again. Rumor was he died of a heart attack at some big convention out East. Thanks to the stranger, I wore the bluing off the little .410 on doves and quail that hunting season and for many seasons to come. Unlike the beautiful Parker, it was a gun I could shoot without worrying about the inevitable nicks and scrapes every upland shotgun receives afield, especially from a young upstart. I also learned that to a birdhunter "beauty is as beauty does" and that the prettiest gun on earth is an empty prize if you can't shoot it.

Like vintage wine, my taste for classic wood and steel has mellowed through the years to encompass some fancy game guns of my own selection. But a crude, hand-polished .410 hammer gun still holds a place of honor in my gun cabinet, a constant reminder of enchanted days and humbler times.

Broomstraw

My first quail hunt, when I was still in bib overalls, taught me more about the natural scheme of things than I was able to cipher from books or basketball. I was eleven, and the single-shot .410 hammer gun I carried afield that gray November day had blistered my thumb from continual cocking practice the evening before. My two older hunting companions, David and Luke, had already graduated to bigger bores. They confidently shouldered 12- and 16-gauge repeaters, and were first to make feathers fly that brisk fall morning.

With military precision we trapped the always-elusive Sulphur Pond covey in the broomstraw between a cut bean field and a shallow creek. "Don't get out in front of us," Luke cautioned me as we marched in on the covey. Suddenly a clump of feathery yellow grass a few yards to my left erupted with a great buzzing of birds. In unison Luke and David yelled for me to shoot. I mounted and fired, but the three-quarter-ounce load of Number 8 shot managed only to fill the empty spaces around the fleeing covey. Two birds fell across the creek, but not to my diminutive gun. With the sweet pungence of burned powder still hanging in the air, we paused a moment to admire the handsome brace of bobwhites. I felt their bean-filled crops, smoothed their delicate feathers, and reluctantly handed them back to my straight-shooting companions. As we spread out across another field, I shivered some from the day's lingering chill but more from the excitement of my first real quail hunt.

The lightweight shotgun I held was a means to an end that day. It carried me through secluded wood lots, over windblown hills, and across fertile grain fields to a place I return to often. It initiated me into a tradition-steeped birdshooting fraternity and launched me on a lifetime of adventure in a natural world that hunters have known for thousands of years.

My first bobwhite was a straggler from a covey that busted out of a honeysuckle tangle that was draped over a tortured line of weather-beaten fenceposts. After the covey rose, all the birds but one veered to the right, and my hunting partners adroitly brought three more to earth. Out of position to shoot, I watched the late-flushing single flutter and sail downhill to a patch of chest-high foxtail. The .410 held at port arms, I slowly approached the weave of dried weeds that sheltered the bobwhite. The spirited single flushed straightaway, and in a motion that seemed strangely second nature, the single-shot reached out with my vision and dropped the quail in a shower of brown feathers. Heart racing, I ran to where I'd marked the bird down. The male bobwhite, its wings spread and still, was cradled in a tuft of grass less than twenty yards from where I had fired. I picked up the plump bird and stood quietly admiring its subtle markings. Somewhere deep inside I knew an age-old rite of passage had been achieved. The event is etched in memory, and I am convinced that had I not hunted that day, that bird and I would never have lived.

On another autumn day during those formative years, I was properly humbled by a veteran birdhunter and a few large coveys that flew unscathed through my gauntlet of gunfire. The first covey we encountered was pinned solidly in the broomstraw by my senior companion's brace of rawboned English pointers—Shy, the larger, and Poke, the bolder. Still encumbered by the naivete of youth, I was about to be treated to a compelling display of classic dog work. Most of my previous quail-hunting adventures were undertaken alone or with an occasional cockle-burred farm dog hunting for a free meal. Closer to the staunch pair than my mentor, I charged in on the point, practically climbing over poor Poke's backside in my zeal to flush the birds. He lurched sideways to sidestep my clumsy intrusion as what seemed like half of southern Illinois's quail population filled the air in front of our faces. In awkward desperation I saluted the huge covey twice without ruffling a feather. I assumed my partner's red face was an expression of embarrassment over my lackluster shooting performance with the double he loaned me. I asked him why he didn't shoot, but was treated only to a headshaking response as he whistled Shy and Poke across a hedgerow and into another field.

After the dogs vacuumed most of a sprawling bicolor patch in spirited English-pointer fashion—completely ignoring my vociferous commands to "hunt 'em up"—both collided simultaneously with the scent of our second covey and stood shivering on point a scant few yards apart. With my eyes riveted to the ground in front of the statuesque pointers, I bumbled in once again, only to have the scattering covey take my hat off as they fled to freedom with the echo of two more poorly pointed volleys reverberating in their little gallinaceous ears. In all the excitement I didn't hear Shy yelp when my knee connected with his rib cage as I danced into shooting position. However, I did manage to hear my gentleman companion mutter a hurried phrase under his breath as we moved on in search of more birds.

The third covey that day was the *coup de grâce*. Poke nailed it tight at the edge of a silage cut and a brushy ravine. With fierce determination I set my eyes on the thick weed patch in front of the dog and marched in on the point. I cut straight in front of Shy, who was gallantly honoring his bracemate's contorted but graceful point. This time the covey wasn't the only thing that exploded from the cover. The birds flushed, I saluted them twice, then disgustedly lowered my smoking double just as my hunting partner dusted me with a barrage of earthy expletives that still bring color to my sallow cheeks. "You stupid oaf!" he yelled, among other things. "If I wasn't so fond of your old man, your backside would be peppered with

Herb Booth

rock salt. Not only is your comportment around gun dogs deplorable, but your self-professed ability as a wingshot is highly suspect." I cringed like a whipped dog as he unloaded his pent-up wrath on my tender young ears. After he settled down a little and made me share my skimpy lunch with Shy and Poke, as a conciliatory gesture, he reviewed a few of the finer points of quail-hunting etiquette with me.

"Son, you never, I mean *never*, walk up the back of a dog on point. Walk well to one side or the other so the dog can see all the action. He certainly can't do it if you're breathing down his neck. And unless you want to risk a perforated rear end, never call down on another man's bird dogs. Keep your mouth shut and watch the dogs work."

"But, but . . . " I stammered.

"No buts about it," he continued. "I promised your dad I'd teach you a few things about birdhunting that might make a sportsman out of you, hopeless as it seems, and I'm goin' to keep my word."

I slowly slouched back against a pin-oak stump and took my whipping like a man. I learned that if I wanted to effectively pick out birds on a covey rise, I would have to focus my eyes on the horizon as I moved in on point and not at the ground directly in front of the dogs. Such an approach prevents you from becoming momentarily disoriented when the panicked covey breaks cover. I was also instructed to take more time when the birds flush, pick a target, mount my double and fire, then drop the stock from my shoulder slightly, locate another bird, remount, and shoot as soon as the stock touched my shoulder pocket. I listened intently as he poured out sage advice that only a dedicated quail hunter could give. Later that afternoon I watched him and his proud dogs put on an unforgettable quail-hunting display. Before the day ended, I even managed to bag a brace of bobwhites. From that day forward, Uncle John, my unselfish instructor, shared his wisdom and his dogs with me and my friends for many bird seasons to come.

The little .410 hammer gun I carried during those upstart years, though its drop dimensions were too great and its length of pull was too short for a gangly adolescent, possessed something that took me half a lifetime to rediscover. It was light and handy. It responded to instinct without hesitation and was quick to the shoulder after a long day of trudging the game fields.

But as they are wont to do, youth and human nature often subscribe to the notion that bigger must always be better. Through late adolescence and early adulthood, I worked my way up the gauges until nothing less than 1¼ ounces of chilled shot in a 12-gauge was sufficient fodder for quail. Bigness of gun and quantity of birds went hand in hand while the weight of the ponderous autoloader I carried slowly wore down my reflexes and my enjoyment in the uplands.

I heard, but did not heed, the old-timers around town who lamented the loss of the well-balanced double guns of yesteryear—those special-order, small-bore Parkers, Foxes, L. C. Smiths, Lefevers, Ithacas, and Remington side-by-sides that had been silenced by the Great Depression and postwar automation. Because most of my shots at upland birds seldom exceed thirty yards, I prefer a gun that can quickly and instinctively be brought to shoulder. Some of my peers still argue that a heavier gun is more forgiving. They say the weight helps with follow-through. I have found that the instinctive style of wingshooting that most birdhunting demands makes a lighter and livelier gun a better choice. When my technique is polished, my arms and upper torso give me all the momentum I need for consistent follow-through. I've adopted the English method of tracking a bird over the top of my gun barrels before completely mounting the shotgun. This fluid motion enables my body to become one with the gun. By tucking the buttstock lightly beneath my armpit with barrels held high, I can pivot to track a bird and be prepared to fire the instant the buttstock touches my shoulder pocket. Because of this time-honored shooting style, English-style game guns seldom tip the scales at more than 6½ pounds in 12-gauge.

As I get older, the wisdom of this lightweight philosophy is especially evident after a long day of pursuing spooky coveys. I've learned the hard way that a 7½-pound shotgun that handles spritely in frost-singed coverts will feel sluggishly cumbersome come sunset. Of course, gun weight can be relative, much of its effect depending on the user's age and physical condition. As a youngster I scoffed at the advice of silver-haired birdhunters. But as time inexorably took its toll on my muscles and reflexes, I began gravitating toward game guns in the six-pound range. My old friend David never missed an opportunity to extol the virtues of 20- and 28-gauge guns weighing a scant five pounds or less. I must admit that some rugged quail terrain makes me wish I were carrying a magic wand, but an ultra-lightweight gun, if not carefully balanced, is difficult for me to control. With traditional one-ounce field loads, such a featherweight gun can also deliver a substantial jolt to the shoulder.

Herb Booth

In addition to favoring well-balanced, "between-the-hands" double guns, I believe quail hunting requires a special reverence for the birds and the habitat that provides them with food and shelter. I have long dreamed of coursing a proud pair of black-and-white mules and a gunning wagon through stately loblolly pines in pursuit of the fabled quail-per-acre experience. Lacking close ties to blue blood and unable to afford shooting britches with bottomless financial pockets, I guess I will have to continue relying on obliging landowners to indulge my love of birdhunting. Whether hunting on private or public land, I always make it a point to study the birds' feeding habits and cover preferences before assembling "old reliable."

Whenever I recall my first bird hunt with Uncle John, I realize what a great teacher humility can be. Even with all my fancy guns and gear, quail continue to humble me, especially when they're all balled up on the edge of a thick woods, or tucked in tight on the far bank of an overgrown drainage ditch, or flushing unexpectedly on a sparsely covered hillside. Older now, earning a livelihood on the seat of my pants, I still draw spiritual sustenance through the soles of my feet as I trek the uplands. While pursuing these spirited buff-colored birds, I see the wisdom of nature's handiwork and the folly of taking myself, or life, too seriously. I know now that I am no more or less a part of the earth's grand scheme than a quail gleaning November grain. Hunting these fascinating birds has taught me to respect their existence as well as my own.

Sixteen Ounces

I watched him break open the vintage shotgun and slip in a pair of low-brass shells. He traced arthritis-gnarled fingers down the file-cut rib to remove an off-season's accumulation of lint and dust. During dormancy the sleek double had hung on wall-mounted pegs above a distressed roll-top desk in his disheveled den. He liked having the gun in full view. It was a visual crutch to help him through the long, empty months between bird seasons. Like the age spots on his hands, the barrels of the trim side-by-side were blotched here and there with superficial brown rust and faint bloodstains. The muzzle of its right barrel was worn thin by three generations of quail hunters in his beloved southland. He was the last of his bloodline.

With trembling hands and a halting, stroke-altered voice, he presented the old gun to me. "Here, boy," he drawled, "bring me home a brace of birds for supper." He gave me a handful of roll-crimped 16-gauge shells and, with rheumy eyes, waved me on into the sedgefield behind his house. Barely fifteen years old, I didn't fully understand the old man's attachment to that gun. After all, he owed me for a summer's worth of grass cutting, and the old double seemed a fair enough swap to me.

Only later in life would I fully realize the significance of his selfless gesture. In time his deep affection for the 16 and quail hunting would become one with my own. A widower without children, the old gentleman lived to hunt birds, or so it seemed. I was his last link with the quail fields and a sporting world that had given joy and substance to his life.

Later that fall he passed away, just about the time I began hitting birds consistently with two barrels and two triggers. Perhaps there is just a touch of sentiment attached to my predilection for 16-gauge double guns. I will certainly never forget the old man and the seductive aroma of those paper shells he gave me that day. Somehow, today's shotshells just don't emanate the same sweet perfume. A few years ago, the old side-by-side was returned to its maker and has been restored to the broomsedge for another generation or two. I like to think that every time a bird falls in front of it the eternal twinkle in the old man's eyes grows a little brighter.

That first double ushered in a lifelong quest for the perfect bird gun. A year later I took my first step on the journey. Just sixteen, I was about to be enticed into trading off a perfectly good Model 12 in 16-gauge. While scanning our county advertiser I came across a classified ad that read: "For Sale— Rare Parker 16 hammer gun. Will trade for pump or semi-auto." Curious, I mustered the courage to make the call. The woman who answered the phone had been well trained by her husband. "You better hurry, young man," she said. "This phone's been ringin' off the hook for that gun. My husband gets off work about 4:30. You better get over here early."

I parked my rusted Chevy across the street from the house about 4 P.M. and waited. Shortly thereafter an old pickup rattled into the driveway and a man with a coal-dusted face and beat-up lunch pail emerged. I hailed him from across the street, and his blinking white eyes followed me as I strode into his front yard. "Came to see the gun," I blurted. He set his pail down on the front porch steps and led me to the workshop behind his house. The gun was cased in a worn-out leg-o'-mutton. He removed the barrels and buttstock and placed them on his workbench. Without saying a word, he unlatched the fore-end from the barrels and assembled the gun. "It was my grandpa's," he announced quietly as he handed me the old hammer gun. Its case colors had long since abandoned the frame and sidelocks, and the long barrels wore a strange shade of brown. Surprisingly, the action still locked up tight. In spite of its crooked stock, the straight-hand gun had that lively feel inherent only to side-by-sides. I broke open the gun, pointed the barrels at the window, and peered down the bores.

"Grandpa pissed down the barrels to rough 'em up," the man said as I squinted, unbelieving, to find any mirrored surface among the pits. "Said they'd pattern better that way," he added while I inspected the peculiar chain-like design on the outside of the barrels. The gun had character, all right, and if I had possessed any at that age, I would have turned on my heels and left "grandpa's gun" in the workshop.

Hopelessly overcome with nostalgia for the "good ole days," I traded my "Perfect Repeater" for the "Gay Nineties" gun. After we'd made the swap, his wife invited me in for some coffee and cake. We talked well into the supper hour before I left for home with my compelling piece of American history. I should have known I had been snookered when none of the other "callers" showed up to look at the gun. At sixteen, I was long on saved-up dollars and short on good sense.

In the months that followed, I put every 16-gauge shell I could find through the gun. When dove season finally opened, I burned through a case of shells I'd found tucked away in the back corner of a termite-ridden general store that was wasting away on a forlorn country crossroads. Discolored and paper-cracked, the high-brass Number 6s were more than the doves or the gun really needed. As I tried fruitlessly to coordinate the intersection of shot string and acrobatic dove, nothing fell off the gun and it didn't blow up in my face. The doves were having their way with me, but I kept bending the hammers back. Even as a bulletproof youngster of sixteen, I had a nagging suspicion I was pushing my luck.

Shoulder-weary and down to my last box of shells, I decided to call it quits. As I was leaving the dove field, I met up with a fellow hunter who asked to see my still-hot sixteen.

"Where did you find this old-timer?" the well-dressed southern gentleman asked as he broke open his beautifully embellished hammerless L. C. Smith and laid it gently on the ground. "Haven't seen one like this in quite some time. You wouldn't want to part with it, would you?"

"Well," I said, reflecting on my abysmal performance with the gun, "if you really want it, maybe we can work out a deal."

"I have a pristine Lefever 16 back at my car I would be willing to trade even up," he offered. When I saw and hefted the gracefully side-plated Lefever, the old hammer gun was his. We talked guns and loads by his car until the late-afternoon sun began to sink below the standing corn. Before we parted, he said I should stick with modern guns and ammunition. He told me to take the Lefever to a gunsmith he knew in town to have it checked out.

Later that week, I did as the gentleman had suggested and visited the gunsmith. While examining the Lefever, the gunsmith mentioned that a man had dropped by earlier in the week and given him an old 16-gauge hammer gun. Said he wanted its firing pins removed before some youngster got hurt with it. Said the gun's Damascus barrels were an accident waiting to happen. I listened, wide-eyed, as the gunsmith detailed the perils of Damascus barrels, and I knew then just how much a gentleman my fellow dove hunter really was.

I shot the Lefever 16 for many seasons to come. Each time I pulled it from its case, I remembered the distinguished gentleman who saved me from myself. I have seldom left a dove field since without looking over my shoulder for a well-dressed guardian angel carrying a heavenly looking L. C. Smith.

As I grew into adulthood, I read endless testimonials in outdoor tabloids touting 12- and 20-gauge guns. The 16 was losing its luster among a new generation of shooters. But if I were limited to only one gauge and one gun for the uplands, it would still be a 16-gauge side-by-side. Given the right chokes, it will throw an ounce of birdshot more efficiently than either the 12 or 20. The 16-gauge, after all, was designed specifically to handle one-ounce loads.

As I continued to research the origins of the 16-gauge, I discovered that the English were the most thorough in their experimentation with shotgun gauges, borings, and loads. Such storied gun houses as Purdey, Holland & Holland, Grant, Lang, Westley

Richards, and others have long recognized the virtues of the 16 gauge. In an early catalog (circa 1928), Westley Richards touted the merits of its New Model 16 Bore: "With improved boring, uniform pattern, and consistent performance, these weapons make effective and handy substitutes for the ordinary 12-bore gun." The Westley Richards 16, with ¼ ounce of Number 6 English shot, delivered an average of 145 to 150 pellets into a thirty-inch circle at forty yards— quite impressive results by anyone's standards. The special chokes for this six-pound, 28-inch-barreled 16 double were not divulged by the gunmaker. British gunmakers especially prefer to keep such wizardry veiled in secrecy. As further testament to the adequacy of its small bores, Westley Richards in the early 1930s offered the following quote from Her Grace the Duchess of Bedford: "A small bore gives the average woman a better chance of holding her own with the 12-bore generally used by men. The charge I have found most suitable for a 16-bore is 35 grains of Amberite, and one ounce of N. 5½-shot. My own gun weighs about 5¾ pounds, which is less than many 20-bores."

In 1924 Holland & Holland claimed that its Special 16 Bore Gun, with its new system of boring (known, of course, only to H & H), was capable of producing similar pattern dispersion at both twenty and forty yards. The following comment concerning this gun appeared in *The Field*, a well-respected publication in England: "Messrs. Holland, in submitting the gun, drew special attention to a curious characteristic which the right barrel possessed to a remarkable extent. They claim in fact to have arrived at a system of boring guns which combines an unusual amount of spread at the near distances with relatively great closeness at forty yards." I wonder where this kind of ballistic alchemy is today. Holland & Holland went on to say that *The Field* test was conclusive proof that its "new" 16-bore patterns were more effective at game ranges and "the equality with 12-bore dispersion is fully established."

Herb Booth

James Purdey & Sons of London has been crafting high-quality double guns for more than 150 years. I have often daydreamed about owning a firearm with the same appeal and performance of a Stradivarius. Given the opportunity, I would revel in playing with a Purdey 16 on released birds in Carnegie Hall. The renowned firm offers two types of 16-gauge guns. Purdey's traditional 16-gauge game gun is built around 2½-inch chambers and, with 27-inch barrels, weighs only 5 pounds 14 ounces. To appease American and European tastes, Purdey also makes a side-by-side for 2¾-inch cartridges that weighs in at an even 6 pounds with 27-inch tubes. Either gun, tailored to my personal dimensions, would heighten my delusions of grandeur in the uplands. The weight of these classic doubles is also perfectly proportioned to respond effortlessly and absorb the recoil of light field loads.

Before I reached legal age I learned that chamber length must always be carefully evaluated when purchasing older 16 doubles from England, Europe, and America. In my late teens I made another potentially disastrous mistake—feeding 2¾-inch shells into chambers only 2 9/16 inches in length. Thankfully, a close friend enlightened me before I blew off a hand, or worse. Many early American doubles were built with such chambers, before 2¾-inch loads became standard. Fortunately, because of the abundance of steel used in many of these older Yankee doubles, a competent gunsmith can ream the shorter chambers to the 2¾-inch length without endangering proof. As 2½-inch shotshells become more readily available, the need to lengthen chambers becomes less worrisome. However, I firmly believe that chambers of lightweight English game guns built and proofed around 2½-inch cartridges should not be lengthened. If they are, they should be sent back to the maker (or other competent gunmaker) for the work and then reproofed at a government proof house in either London or Birmingham. As my friend so eloquently impressed upon me, excessive pressures generated by maximum-loaded 2¾-inch shells in 2½-inch-chambered game guns is a fate not worth tempting.

Headspacing is another minor, but sometimes annoying, idiosyncrasy I have experienced with older American doubles. Because the brass on turn-of-the-century shotshell rims was somewhat thicker than today's offerings, that mysterious rattle I often heard in some of my older guns was usually nothing more than the cartridge head tapping back against the standing breech. My gunsmith assured me this trait poses no serious threat to the shooter or the gun beyond an insignificant increase in recoil. To ensure the natural onset of more gray hair, though, I make sure every used double I bring home is inspected by my gunsmith before I dirty the barrels.

In Europe the 16-gauge still enjoys considerable popularity. Various French, Belgian, and Spanish gunmakers offer it in both boxlock and sidelock configurations. The prices are often very reasonable considering that many of the gunmakers will build a gun to suit the customer's individual requirements. One fall I flirted with an attractive French Darne. With its unique sliding breech, it was a very svelte, quick-handling side-by-side in 16-gauge. Numerous Liege gunmakers also cater to the Europeans' desire for 16-gauge doubles. In my book, the best value for the money in double guns is offered by Spain's Old-World gun trade. These dedicated craftsmen have faithfully copied the painstaking process of "putting up guns" in the best English tradition. In fact, a great percentage of Eibar's annual double-gun production is exported to the shooting gentry of Great Britain.

To my everlasting chagrin, some gunmakers have built 16-gauge guns around 12-gauge frames. Along with hampering the unique handling dynamics of the 16, such frame tampering ultimately sealed the fate of the 16 in the U.S., although the reverse of this equation can be rewarding. I briefly waltzed with a delightful 16-gauge VH Parker that was built on an O frame (Parker's 20-gauge frame). It was light and fast, but, thanks to its excessive drop at comb and heel, it kicked like hell. Confronted with ever-rising production costs, American gunmakers eventually dropped the 16 in favor of the highly touted 20-gauge. Had the 16 received the same press in the emerging clay-target games (especially skeet) as did the 12- and 20-gauges, it may have survived the Depression and the merciless scrutiny of the corporate bean-counters. With the demise of the American double, a lot of the romance of shooting was lost as the sporting press beat a path to the "high-tech," "how-to" school of journalism.

Unlike many latter-day American sporting arms, most European 16-gauge game guns have barrel centers and frames scaled to the proper dimensions. Frame size dictates the thickness and contour of the barrels, the strength of the water table, the size of the locks, underlugs, etc.

My years of experience with the gauge have demonstrated that uniform patterns and short shot strings are usually characteristics of a quality 16 double. The length of a $^{15}/_{16}$ or one-ounce shot column in relation to the 16's bore diameter not only reduces bore scrub but also minimizes the deformation of shot as they engage the choke. Such "square" loads produce in-the-field ballistics that bring joy to every birdhunter's heart. To take full advantage of barrel-forcing cones, I prefer to use shells without plastic sleeves or cups. I reload my game loads with fiber wads when I can find them. They guarantee a consistent gas seal at all temperatures and do not leave a plastic legacy in the game fields for future hunters to lament. Although there is some pellet deformation with unprotected shot columns, full advantage is taken of forcing cones and chokes. Needless to say, such wads and shotshells are as scarce as vestal virgins.

For early season quail, woodcock, and grouse over dogs, I prefer Eley's 2½-inch, 2½-dram shell loaded with $^{15}/_{16}$ of an ounce of Number 9 shot. The load leaves a lot of powder residue in the barrel, but its downrange performance is impressive. As the season progresses, I load my left barrel with an ounce of Number 8 or 7½ shot pushed by 2¾ drams of powder. Although it is a tad light, many a boisterous ringneck has hit the ground fluttering from this load's deadly sting. Experience afield has taught me that heavy loads and large shot belong more in the duck blind and less in the uplands.

There will always be those who herald short barrels for birds in thick cover, but I think that barrels of 27 to 29 inches in length make a 16 side-by-side handle and perform in a lively fashion. I have found they also provide balance and pointability that shorter barrels just can't match, and I don't ever recall bouncing them off bark in my attempts to down birds.

Battle-scarred New England partridge hunters and buggy-bred southern birdshooters have known all along that the 16-gauge double is the preferred medicine for buff-colored birds. Lighter than a 12, more graceful than a 20, the 16's ounce of prevention is indeed worth a pound of cure in the uplands, at least to my way of thinking. Lord have mercy on those unenlightened souls who believe their roaring 12s and overfed 20s are deadlier than sin on all manner of gamebirds. But then again, maybe their guardian angels don't hunt doves.

Birds of a Feather

The defiant barn was all that remained of a Depression-ravaged farm. It wasn't much to look at, but it had potential. Its hand-hewn timbers, cracked from years of holding up abundant harvests, were a testament to its German architects. I unlocked and swung open the sagging barn door, swept aside the cobwebs, and tried to peer into the future.

"Get serious," Luke contested. "Do ya really think the boys'll want to turn this heap into a huntin' shack?" I gave him a cold stare and shuffled deeper into the musty darkness of the old barn.

"Uncle John said we can get this place for a song," I sang out with authority. "The least we can do is give it the once over."

Swifts had moved into what once passed for a fieldstone chimney on the north end of the structure. Luke picked up a weathered ax handle and raked a skein of mud-dauber houses off one of the walls. "Looks like the critters. . . ."

"Take a look at this, Luke," I interrupted. "Come over here and help me lift off this tarp." I had stumbled across a large bedraped object in a back corner. We cautiously tugged on the dropping-laden canvas and unveiled a green and black 1929 Nash, complete with wool upholstering, sturdy running boards, and wooden spoke wheels. Its dark paint was faded and checked, but the massive body was free of dents and rust.

"If it runs, it'll make a great huntin' wagon," Luke said beaming. "Wonder if it comes with the farm?"

"Don't know," I responded, "but I wouldn't be surprised if the trunk was full of bootleg whiskey."

Luke and I poked around the lonely building for more than an hour, filled an old UMC ammo box with a few glass telephone-line insulators we found sequestered on a window sill, then headed for home. We were anxious to tell our comrades in arms about the new gathering place. As if to consummate the deal, a bobwhite whistled its approval in the gathering dusk when we exited the barn. We jumped in Luke's knobby-tired Jeep and sped down the rutted dirt lane toward the hard road.

The location of the abandoned farmstead was just what we had in mind—far enough out of town to give it a country feel, but close enough for us to make a beer run every now and then. Barring a population explosion, it would give us a private place to plan hunting strategies, swap tall tales, and resist the ever-more-feminine constraints of modern civilization.

"It's a place where you can scratch where it itches," Luke told Uncle John as we discussed our findings with the kindred flock on his sprawling front porch. Uncle John always had his fingers on the pulse of our small town, and very little life went on that escaped his scrutiny. A decorated Korean War vet without sons of his own, he had more or less adopted us as part of his family. Frank and David, hunting partners since childhood, grinned with anticipation, then began firing questions about what was needed to fix the place up. Frank was our army surplus quartermaster, and before anyone dared send off to some fancy mail-order catalog for a new piece of hunting gear, he had better have checked with Frank first. Frank's brother-in-law moonlighted as manager of the county salvage yard—meaning our local hardware store was going to be hard-pressed to make any money off our barn-raising venture. David, purist-minded and articulate, was our "shady tree" legal beagle, and we sent him chasing down any property liens or other encumbrances before we bought the farm. Mark, the youngest of the gathering, wanted to know if his bird dogs could have the run of the place.

Within a few months the old barn was sanitized, manicured, and wired for light. Frank scrounged an antique, chrome-trimmed, potbellied stove from his brother-in-law. He had to win a pitched battle with his wife for the relic before we could wrestle it into its position of prominence in the gathering place. We ruined three lengths of store-bought stovepipe before making a connection with the barn's freshly tuck-pointed chimney. Luke said he didn't want any prying eyes violating our hideaway when we were gone, so shutters were attached to the building's four windows—one set for each point on the compass. Nailing into the dry oak was like trying to convince Uncle John that 20-gauges were genuine bird guns or persuading Luke that Gordon setters were honest-to-goodness bird dogs. The original square spikes securing timber to beam had no doubt been driven in with sledges by work-hardened men of a lost generation who took the world as they found it, abiding by the natural law of the land.

With a summer's worth of sweat equity and a few minor altercations over "interior design," the old barn was given a new lease on life. At last we had a secluded place to escape from the workaday world. At our first real gathering, David offered up a short but inspiring invocation to the great Creator of frosty mornings, strong bird scent, staunch dogs, and endless seasons. During his brief prayer the far-off sound of migrating geese pierced the edifice, lifting spirits all around.

"Load up the huntin' wagon!" Luke commanded. "It's time we popped a few caps at some clay birds in the back forty." Festooned with cased guns, assorted bird dogs, and a full complement of eager shooters, the rebuilt twelve-cylinder Nash groaned under the strain but dutifully chugged its cargo out to the shoot-

ing grounds. Capone and his henchmen never rode in grander style. Ground clearance on the vintage auto allowed us to span furrows and straddle boulders as we bumped down fencerows and across open fields to the small, played-out gravel pit that would serve as our clay-target range. During the dusty trek Luke pounced on a still-sealed crock that rolled out from under the front seat and flashed a mischievous grin. Uncle John wrestled the jug away for safekeeping. With the lure of its contents dominating Luke's one-track mind, our sojourn turned out to be a short one. Satisfied with our clay-busting performance, Luke gathered us into the car for a quick, bone-jarring ride back to the gathering place. We broke

Herb Booth

more targets in the trunk of the gyrating Nash than we had at the pit. Nighthawks dive-bombed the cloud of insects left in our wake as we transacted the winter wheat stubble in our dash back to the barn.

What transpired around the potbellied stove during that first gathering was pure rapture. We ran out of earthy palaver before the jug could be emptied of its magical elixir, and randomly sprawled, stupefied and sleep-filled, about the barn. When we returned bleary-eyed to our domiciles early the next morning, the stories we told our loved ones reduced our previous night's prevarications to child's play. It was the beginning of a ritual that would be repeated many times at the gathering place.

Mortgaging our time with rod and gun around vernal and autumnal equinoxes, the years melted away all too swiftly: fall's colorful raiment whipped bare by winter's inevitable winds and sleet, spring's refreshing breath suffocated by summer's unstoppable heat and humidity. The old barn, ever resistant to change, weathered the seasons well. Those of us who gathered there accepted our lot in life, each trying to cheat fate out of just one more good bird dog, or another double on a covey rise, or a late-night "whopper swapper" around the hissing stove.

Life in our sleepy little corner of the world caught an incurable dose of hurry sickness when the foreign car factory moved into town. Its corporate tentacles quickly spread across the agrarian countryside, controlling the flux and flow of men and materials, interrupting the natural scheme of things. In our soon-to-be subdivided back forty, fewer and fewer quail whistled up the coming of spring or the fall of night. Civilization was crowding in. The old barn, a survivor of empty harvests and hard times, was now trapped in a prosperity it could not outlive. Like ghosts, we haunted the enchanted place until the real world cast us adrift from one another. Uncle John, Luke, David, Frank, Mark, and I all longed for one last hunt together, one more friendly meeting at the gathering place.

Luck of the Irish

Baron McDuff pushed his seven-week-old nose through the dog run's cyclone fencing and gnawed affectionately on my forefinger. I wasn't aware of it then, but before day's end the tawny Irish curse would be curled up in my lap on his way to a new home. I ventured to Fieldcrest Kennels that warm summer morning seeking a chocolate, yellow, or black Lab to assist in my autumnal pursuits of barnyard-size pheasants and plump northern mallards. The Lab, I had been advised by my duck-hunting friend Frank, was a gun dog that could hunt both with ease. Frank assured me that a big black Lab or one of its color variations, stalwart in the field and companionable at home, was the only logical choice.

Had I possessed the wisdom that years bring and the savvy of a seasoned dog man, I would have coolly resisted the needle-toothed Irish-setter imp tugging on my pant leg. Certainly, I would have heeded all the talk tossed around about the high-strung, obstinate qualities innate in the Irish breed and settled for nothing less than a Lab. The pitiful little puppy would probably have charmed a more deserving master had I not asked the trainer to let the frisky "Golden Retriever" out of the dog run.

I was far from an authority on dog flesh, except maybe for some of the peculiar antics of those face-licking mongrels that chased neighborhood cats during my childhood years. And I soon began to sense the seriousness of my hasty decision to make the setter a part of my life. I should have brought young Mark with me that day. Gifted since childhood, he had a sixth sense about bird dogs. If I brought home a "biscuit eater," he'd never let me live it down. The thought of raising an honest-to-goodness bird dog from scratch had an unexpectedly intimidating effect on me. However, during the long drive home I rationalized that it was about time I had my own bird dog. Considering the amount of time I spent in uplands each fall, the Irish setter should work out well enough.

As the weeks of night-crying gradually subsided, Duffy's domain expanded from our kitchen to our backyard, where my initiation into setter rearing took on a whole new dimension. Whatever there is in a male setter's urine that can render perfectly healthy sod into dust-slick ground overnight ought to be isolated for use by the military as a defoliant. This biological phenomenon, coupled with my setter's trenching ability, about sealed his fate as a volunteer for the canine corps—and made McDuff and my spouse (a.k.a. the "war department") about as compatible as Vibram-soled boots and dog dung.

When it comes to women and bird dogs, it is an understatement to say that first impressions can be somewhat important. Unfortunately, as quickly as my childless wife was taken in by the frisky pup, her antique furniture was taken out for repairs. Duffy's teeth and toenails disfigured pine, oak, and walnut without prejudice. Mark told me to hide my Russell boots and anything else of value from the dog. The incorrigible setter also had an affinity for lamp cords, patent leather, and roasts left to cool on the kitchen counter.

But what Duffy lacked in decorum around the house, he more than compensated for with his desire to hunt in the field. During our weekend runs at the gathering place, no cover was too thick to be explored by the Duff. He vaulted, bulldozed, and busted brush better than many of the shorthaired pointing dogs I'd hunted with over the years. Strong-boned and thick-skinned, he was a natural for the rigors of upland work. Watching him cover ground with his feathery tail held high like a scimitar was a source of joy well worth the occasional torment of chasing after him with whistle and whip.

As the weeks progressed and Duffy's obedience afield didn't, I knew I would have to assign his training to someone more gifted than myself. Friend Mark, no doubt weakened by my summer-long hangdog look, and perhaps out of some residual feelings of guilt for not volunteering to help me start a new dog, agreed to give McDuff a September's worth of field work. There is more than a little truth to the saying "Bend a sapling when it is young": Mark's effect on my year-old setter was both dramatic and permanent. In a few short weeks he brought out in Duffy what months of my best backyard intentions had yet to accomplish, training books notwithstanding. I'm sure Mark's innate understanding of bird dogs and infinite patience had a lot to do with it, but McDuff's indomitable spirit was also an important factor. He was pointing staunchly and retrieving birds like fabled dogs I had often read about but seldom got the privilege to hunt over.

With all animals of noble lineage and character, proper breeding is essential. McDuff's Irish dame was a deep-chested huntress from Limerick, Ireland, while his sire was a high-tailed hunter from Wisconsin—a match conceived by mortals but mixed with sufficient doses of the Emerald Isle's magic and blended with a drop of the American Dream. Baron McDuff embraced the best of both worlds, and I hoped the luck of the Irish and my latent Yankee ingenuity would keep him in plenty of birds throughout his seasons.

Duff's true test afield came in the fall of his second season. Nonplussed as I was about his developing fondness for exploring horizons around the back forty, I departed for Iowa's heartland with fellow birdhunters Frank and David. Pen-reared birds and a few obliging wild quail had filled McDuff's nose with bird scent and coaxed some stylish points, but the wild-flushing Iowa pheasants would provide a challenging test for the mahogany dog. Before I left on the trip, Uncle John, true to form, chided me about traveling all the way to Iowa to "campaign a foreign dog on imported ditch parrots, especially in the middle of bird season."

More than once during the daylong journey to the Iowa cornfields, my two longtime hunting partners tactfully broached the subject of Irish-setter behavior in general and McDuff's development in particular. It seems they, too, had read some of the bad press about the Irish setter's hunting credentials. I explained that Duffy's genealogy differed considerably from that of Irish setters bred for the bench. McDuff's parents were both field-bred Irish setters registered in the American Kennel Club and the Field Dog Stud Book (which substantiates field bloodlines).

Herb Booth

My partners also knew full well what Mark could do with a bird dog.

After copious dog, gun, and hunting conversation, we arrived at our Iowa destination late in the afternoon, bought our licenses, and drove to the farm we would hunt the next morning. The station wagon fishtailed up the farmer's rutted clay driveway made slippery by a somber November drizzle, scattering a flock of squawking guinea fowl that announced our arrival. The farmer was a crusty old-timer of past acquaintance whose only tariff for our morning's hunt would be a tender, field-dressed cockbird.

A light frost clung to the cornstalks the next morning. After some small talk with our friendly farmer, we made straight for the fields to consummate our part of the bargain with our host. Cows were in the cut corn, so we decided to make an upwind swing through a sprawling alfalfa field that stretched to the western horizon. Duffy's ears perked when my Parker snapped closed on the birdshot. He nuzzled closer to my pant leg and sat trembling in anticipation of my command to "Hunt 'em up!"

My favorite hunting socks scarcely had time to crawl down into my boots before Duffy began winding birds. He was casting between me and my companions, tail held high, about forty yards out. Not accustomed to finding birds in such sparse-looking cover, we were all surprised by McDuff's first point that morning. From the way the bird was holding, I expected a hen to flush and was completely surprised by the two raucous roosters that catapulted into the sun. Anxious to down a bird for my dog, I insulted him and my Parker by smoking both barrels without touching a feather. Luckily, David, nonplussed as always, managed to bag the late-flushing younger bird for McDuff and the farmer. Duffy was quickly on the fluttering pheasant and sauntered past my partners to give me the colorful bird. I reassured my friends that the dog wasn't being insolent but rather that Mark had trained him to retrieve only for his master. However, I couldn't help wonder if McDuff was rubbing it in some when he circled me a couple of times before sitting to deliver the pheasant.

My next opportunity came in late afternoon. Frank and David, their game bags already filled to the limit, were lending moral support as I hustled down a fencerow to where McDuff was locked on point. Cackling defiantly, a large cockbird broke cover a few feet from my dog's nose, cleared the fence, and sped out over a bean field, where my second load of Number 7½ shot finally caught up with him. Evidence of Duffy's bird-finding prowess already bouncing against their backsides, my lifelong compatriots needed no further convincing of his pointing or retrieving abilities. But as if to allay any lingering doubts about the hunting aptitude of a properly bred and trained Irish setter, McDuff bounded over the four-foot-high sheep fence, retrieved the pheasant, then jumped the fence again and delivered the bird to hand. I looked around as if it was all in a day's work, knelt, and kissed my dog on the muzzle. Now, all of this may sound as if I am overworking the truth a bit, but if a man doesn't occasionally brag on his bird dog or his kids, he really deserves neither.

With little prompting from me, the conversation on our trip home was punctuated by more than a few testimonials to at least one red dog's ability to please his master. Knowing full well I would be redressed by Uncle John when we returned, I asked my friends to enlighten him at our next gathering about McDuff's command performance.

That Iowa hunt was indeed a red-setter day—one I will remember every time McDuff races out of earshot, gooses a house guest, bumps a bird, points a skunk, rolls in a cow plop, dines on garbage, or does any of the other mischievous things an honest-to-goodness hunting dog is inclined to do.

Through no expertise of my own, and with Mark's capable guidance, McDuff has conquered his wanderlust. He has even learned to hunt close in among the few thornapple-choked woodcock coverts near the gathering place. I suppose he has done more than a little training on me as well, because I no longer expect him, or myself, to perform flawlessly afield. I have accepted his limitations as much as he has mine, and together we are beginning to make a fairly effective hunting team. So much so, in fact, that whenever I encounter another hunter in the uplands and watch him cast a baleful glance at my dog and then me, I no longer seek distant fields but just hope the infidel stays close enough to get an eyeful of Irish dog work as it was meant to be. I know there will always be those like Uncle John who say no mollycoddled, home-kept hunting dog will ever amount to much in the field, least of all an Irish setter. Despite such unwarranted slander, I will always love McDuff like a son and hunt him like the true hunter he is, a flaming torch of his Irish heritage and a capable bird dog by any American standard.

Fit to Shoot

It was one of those easy, open straightaway shots, the kind grouse hunters dream about but seldom get. My intrepid setter had done his job, pinning down the large drummer at the edge of a power line right-of-way. Now it was time to do mine. With great certainty of action, I cheeked the old double and ignited the right barrel. The fleeing grouse never flinched. In disbelief, I desperately groped for the rear trigger. It had the same effect on the gray blur. I lowered the gun, gave it an incredulous look, then sheepishly glanced over at my dog. "Well, boy," I apologized, "you've just watched a skilled wingshot turn into a horse's ass." Those two shots hounded me for days as I brooded over the incident, trying to identify the glitch that embarrassed me in front of my dog.

For years, romance, not reason, ruled the roost at my house when it came to upland birdhunting. Stock dimensions and patterning boards were lost in my quest for turn-of-the-century, O-framed Parkers and pristine paper-hulled shells. A fit gun to me was a small-bore Fox, or a pre-1913 L. C. Smith, or a high-grade Lefever, or any other grand old American-made double gun. Never mind their archaic stock dimensions or the fact that my six-foot, four-inch frame required custom-tailored clothing, so long as the guns were covered in proper patina and steeped in sporting nostalgia. As a result, each gun in my repertoire required a different series of contortions before my master left eye could be properly aligned with the rib. Instinctive and consistent gun mounting was always a challenge with the eclectic relics I coveted and collected. Shooting with the vintage guns was strictly a hit-or-miss proposition.

Through years of trial and error, and after relinquishing some romantic but unproductive notions, I finally unlocked the secret to successful shooting. It wasn't some new rib configuration or high-tech sighting gadget or screw-in choke device. Nor was it a switch from classic game guns to over/unders or repeaters. My infatuation with the unheralded and oft-ignored 16-gauge was not the answer either. I did have the good fortune of meeting Andrew, a be-whiskered Englishman who knew his way around a try-gun. In a deliberate flurry of tape measurements and try-gun adjustments one afternoon, he fitted me up with stock dimensions that felt too long, too straight, and too awkward to be of any value afield.

Affable and immaculately attired in crisply pressed khaki, Andrew greeted me in the parking lot of his tree-studded shooting grounds in southern Wisconsin. It was one of those sultry August afternoons with a heat index that could soften antimony shot. Even the trees were looking for shade.

"How was your trip, Richard?" Andrew chirped in his flawless English accent as we entered his cozy, den-like pro shop. "Everything is set on the range. Are you ready to have a go at it?"

In deference to my many seasons of shooting experience, and perhaps sensing I was on the verge of heatstroke, Andrew casually asked me a few questions in the air-conditioned comfort of the shop. "How long have you been shooting from the left shoulder, Richard?" he began.

"Well," I stammered, "ever since I shot my first house sparrow with a Red Ryder. I was about nine years old, I guess."

"You're left-handed, then," he offered.

"Actually, I'm right-handed but always felt more natural shooting from the left shoulder," I said.

"It's not unusual," Andrew advised, "for right-handed individuals to be left-eye dominant. Your left eye directs and controls your vision. That is why shooting from your left shoulder feels natural to you."

Sizing me up all the while with his smiling blue eyes, he fired questions at me in rapid succession, jotting my responses on a notepad. "How tall are you, Richard?"

"Well," I said coyly, "it depends on how I feel, but the tape usually reaches six feet, four inches on good days."

"Chest size?"

"Forty-four inches," I said.

"Sleeve length?"

"Thirty-five inches."

"Neck?"

"Seventeen inches."

"Glove size?"

"Ten."

"That should just about do it," he concluded. Sarcastically, I asked him if there were any other vital statistics he or my wife should be aware of that might affect my shooting. "Only one," he responded, "the size of your ego. It's the one thing that determines the real measure of a man."

We left his cool shop and walked down a path freshly manicured with aromatic wood chips. We soon came to a large clearing that held a makeshift metal backdrop about twenty-five yards downrange from a wooden gun rack. Andrew wrenched adjustments into

the well-worn, 12-gauge double try-gun he carried. It was an unadorned W. & C. Scott boxlock side-by-side. Every so often his bright eyes would flash up at me as he fine-tuned the gun's dimensions.

"Here we go," he said, opening the empty gun and handing it to me. "Now close the gun, mount it swiftly, and point it right at my nose." After years of strict, muzzle-conscious training, I balked at pointing even an empty gun at anyone. He assured me it was all right, and I did as he asked.

"Good! Good!" he said, retrieving the gun once again to increase the length of pull a quarter-inch and raise the comb an eighth. He loaded the right barrel and handed the gun back to me. I shouldered it at the target downrange. It felt strangely awkward, but I was determined to give the try-gun the old college try. While outlining the fine points of instinctive gun mounting, posture and stance, he instructed me to quickly mount and fire at the newly whitewashed metal target board downrange. He studied my mounting technique and watched where the paint flew on my first shot. Within three shots, with gun adjustments made after each, Andrew conformed the gun perfectly to my form. Each subtle refinement, he assured me, would help build in target-hitting consistency afield.

I asked him whether an over/under try-gun would give him the same measurements. "It matters little," he explained, "but grip and fore-end styles do make a difference." He went on to say that straight-hand guns with splinter fore-ends require less drop at the comb and heel than do guns equipped with tight pistol grips and bulbous beavertail forearms.

Once Andrew was satisfied with my performance on the target board, we strolled over to the sporting-clays course that meandered along the high bank of a willow-lined river. As we approached the first station, he instructed me to take a more relaxed stance and strive for a more fluid body motion prior to shouldering the gun. As I was quickly discovering, he was right on target. I broke the first pair of clay birds that raced through the trees.

"Most American shooters make the mistake of taking too wide a stance," Andrew explained. "Such an exaggerated, rigid stance inhibits footwork and weight transfer as the gun is swung through the target. It also causes the shoulder to drop on crossing shots." He pointed out that my feet should form an open-ended V no wider than my hips to help control and balance my body movements. Obviously, this stance seldom works afield, but it has certainly helped me improve my scores on the skeet range and the sporting-clays course.

Andrew's instinctive-style shooting technique taught me that my shoulder is the triggering mechanism, the gun being fired the moment the buttstock makes contact with the shoulder pocket. "This is one of the cardinal rules of instinctive shooting, Richard," Andrew advised, "and whether on targets or game, it demands a gun that fits."

As we moved from station to station, I gave Andrew feedback regarding the fit and feel of the gun. At first the comb felt too high and my leading hand occasionally pulled free of the barrels during recoil. I also told him my index finger was straining to reach the front trigger of the try-gun. He backed off on the length of pull a bit, and my complaints drifted away with the powdered targets.

I soon discovered that the longer, straighter stock locked my head down on the comb of the stock. No more involuntary head-lifting, a nasty habit that has cost me more birds than I would care to count. Andrew informed me that the length of pull on most English game guns averages ½ to 1½ inches longer than on American shotguns. "Longer stocks are well suited to the 'thrust forward' method of gun mounting taught by the British," he told me. "American hunters feel they must quickly slide the stock into place, thinking no doubt that it is the shortest distance to the shoulder. Unfortunately, the buttstock often catches on clothing, botching the shot. Instead of serving the stock up to the cheek, the shooter forces his head down to accommodate the poorly mounted stock. By its very design," Andrew continued, "the English game gun forces the shooter's leading hand to become more than a barrel rest during the process of mounting and firing. This hand must push the gun out from the body, up toward the target, and back into the shoulder pocket in a smooth, almost fluid motion. Once mastered," he announced, "the 'thrust forward' method becomes as natural as pointing your finger."

With my length of pull established, Andrew began to carefully evaluate my try-gun's drop dimensions. He still thought I needed a tad less drop at the comb, so he cranked it up to 1⅛ inches. "Because the comb, as cheek rest, aligns the sight plane of the barrels with the eyes," he explained, "it must be of proper height and shape. A low, thinly tapered comb can be extremely punishing. Such sharp combs are common on American doubles made around the turn of the century. Hunters at that time were taught to keep their heads almost totally erect while shooting."

He also pointed out that the degree of cast built into the buttstock adds comfort and consistency as well. "Cast," Andrew related, "is the distance the buttstock is angled laterally left or right to ensure proper sight alignment and positioning in the shoulder pocket. Again, anatomy dictates proper fit, and I strive to eliminate as many obstacles to instinctive gun mounting as possible."

After I exited the Whistling Woodcock station, my lackluster shooting prompted him to readjust my cast-on to about $3/8$ of an inch. As if to confirm his judgment and restore my confidence, I broke nine out of ten at the next station.

Andrew was the first person to explain shotgun pitch in terms I could understand. "Pitch, or pitch down, usually falls between 0 and 2½ inches on 28-inch-barreled guns," he instructed as he fiddled with the butt adjustment on the try-gun. "Shotguns with a large amount of stock drop and pitch down will pattern shot lower than a gun fitted with a straighter stock." He placed the palm of his left hand flat against the butt, held the gun up in front of him, and showed me the angle of the butt from top to bottom, as it related to the level barrels. It was almost parallel to the plane of the muzzles—0 pitch. "Most English game guns," he continued, "have very little down pitch. This imparts a decidedly upward influence to the barrels when the gun is mounted, offering somewhat of a built-in lead for overhead or flushing birds."

Much to the surprise of both of us, I made a dismal showing at the Wild Quail station. "It appears you still need a little help with your gun mounting, Richard," Andrew said politely. "Remember, the 'thrust forward' gun mount is a three-step procedure. It's really quite simple. First the gun is brought to the ready position, sort of a modified port arms. Then the buttstock is tucked lightly under the armpit with the barrels covering the moving target. Finally, with the body initiating the swing," and here he motioned as if raising and swinging a gun, "the gun is thrust forward slightly to clear the armpit and brought back into the shooting pocket in one quick motion. When the buttstock touches the shoulder, the gun is fired in follow-through form, not unlike a golf, baseball, or cricket swing, if you will. It sounds complicated, but it can be done in the twinkling of an eye once you get the hang of it."

Andrew went on to stress the importance of the leading hand in gun mounting and follow-through. "If your leading hand is placed too far forward on the barrels," he demonstrated, "the gun will have a tendency to shoot high. Conversely, if it is positioned too close to the action, the gun will be inclined to shoot low. As you can see, a well-fit buttstock helps position your leading hand naturally and comfortably on the barrels. Your leading hand," he continued, "can also be used to compensate for poor drop dimensions. If your gun has too much drop, simply slide your leading hand farther down the barrels like this. If the stock is too straight, grip closer to the action body. However, there is still no substitute for a properly fit gun."

Andrew informed me that unless there is some physical abnormality, adult drop and cast dimensions should fall into the following ranges: Drop at Comb, $7/8$ to $1^5/8$ inches; Drop at Heel, $1^7/8$ to $2^1/2$ inches; Length of Pull, $13^7/8$ to 16 inches. Cast Off and Cast On will usually vary from $1/8$ to $3/8$ inches, toe in or out.

"These are general guidelines," Andrew warned. "Every person's anatomy requires a different set of statistics."

Thanks to Andrew's competent and cool instruction, that round of sporting clays was an all-time high for me, oppressive heat notwithstanding. As we sauntered back to the clubhouse, appreciating the canopy of towering trees and a freshening breeze, Andrew gave me a handwritten piece of ivory parchment that detailed my new stock measurements. "These will probably change some as you age," he remarked, draping the open try-gun over his shoulder. "You'll need a touch more drop as Father Time begins reshaping your physique."

After a "spot of tea" I bid Andrew farewell and drove away from his shooting retreat with a new set of stock measurements and a better understanding of gun fit. Within a week of the fitting, after a few practice sessions at the back forty gravel pit, the new stock dimensions became second nature to me. I was consistently hitting targets at every angle, without struggling to fit the gun to my anatomy with each shot. Later that season, grouse began to fall in front of my restocked double gun. In a fit of birdhunter delirium, I went on a restocking rampage that left me with a gun collection I could shoot and a bank account that was completely shot. Looking back, I believe it was a small price to pay for the satisfaction it has given me season after season.

Before the try-gun experience, I had always marveled at the antics of competitive trapshooters. To extract the last ounce of consistency from their customized guns, they continually experiment with comb height, grip shape, and length of pull. Some over-the-counter trap guns even look like modified try-guns with their adjustable comb and length-of-pull stocks.

Years ago, when gamebirds were abundant and bag limits generous, it was possible for hunters, in the course of shooting thousands of rounds, to become proficient marksmen in spite of improper gun fit. Many country boys in my neck of the woods became credible with club-like shotguns that led me to cast some doubt on all this custom gunfitting business. But for every birdhunter who has mastered an ill-fitting stock, there are a hundred more who needlessly torture noses, cheekbones, and lips with thumb-knuckles and stock combs.

The British have long recognized the importance of gun fit. London, Birmingham, and Edinburgh gunmakers would no more attempt to sell me a game gun without first fitting me with a try-gun than a custom tailor would sell me a suit without taking my measurements. To them, fit is foremost. I know one lanky old New England grouse hunter about six feet tall who was measured for a bird gun by a famous gunmaking house in London during World War II. When Uncle Sam brought him home from "across the pond," he asked Winchester to build him a Model 21 20-gauge to the English measurements. At first the New Haven factory protested, claiming that a 16½-inch length of pull was just too long for any man to shoot. In retrospect I wish Winchester had talked him out of those arcane stock measurements. Had they succeeded, scores of New England grouse and woodcock would have survived to fly another day. An old-timer now, he is still deadly with the gun.

Will-O'-the-Wisp

Some very impressive scientific names are attached to that confusion of foliage I usually refer to as brush, undergrowth, or scrub. Because I spent much of my childhood chasing garter snakes, discovering bird nests, and riding down springy saplings, these tangled playgrounds remain havens for my imagination. Whether thornapple, alder, or poplar, these thickets still challenge me with discoveries that temper the prospect of growing old.

Trapped between tollway and railroad tracks just forty minutes north of Chicago, the "city of broad shoulders" near a prairie-state college I attended, there exists an unincorporated thicket that quietly ignores civilization's relentless encroachment. It hosts such fauna as saw-whet owls, white-tailed deer, and, in early fall, woodcock. My Midwestern mind had always pictured the woodcock as a bird steeped in sporting tradition, a will-o'-the-wisp of the tag alders, and patron of New England's rock-walled coverts. Seen only on case-colored double guns and in the yellowing pages of Derrydale books, the strange vision that flushed on the edge of the thicket during an early September dove outing surprised me and my yearling Irish setter. Though I'd been reared on quail and was content with pheasants, my initiation into woodcock hunting would prove a revelation. No other single event, except perhaps my trip to the altar, would change my sporting life so dramatically. This mysterious migrant with misplaced eyes and prehensile beak would challenge my complacent shooting instincts and my setter's pointing ability like no other upland bird.

Seemingly made impatient by a lingering Indian summer, fall moved swiftly through the uplands that October. The weather was unseasonably wet, and the pungency of fermenting leaves and marsh grass scented my first serious effort to gun woodcock. Confused by the bell on his collar and the thick cover, my setter's customary ranginess was held in check as he wove through wiry curtains of puckerbrush, pausing occasionally for me to follow. Rambling briars and low-hanging thornapple branches clawed at my clothing and traced crimson scrolls on my hands and face.

While groping through a sun-dappled thicket, I noticed that the steady ring of my dog's bell had suddenly stopped. Blinded by the thick canopy of tangled vegetation, I dropped to my knees and spotted my dog locked on point a few yards to my left. I threaded my gun's muzzles around and through a maze of undergrowth as I slowly crab-walked and crawled alongside my trembling setter. Still unable to stand, I carefully searched the ground ahead while inching in on the point. Suddenly, as if spat from the earth, a specter of a bird rose on squeaky wings and pirouetted through the copse. I fired from a squat position and watched the Number 8 shot from my cylinder barrel cut a skylight in the skeletal limbs just behind the fleeing woodcock. The recoil rocked me back on my haunches, but I managed a quick shot with my second barrel just as the bird topped out of the cover. The ring in my ears from the roar of the smoothbore was soon replaced by that of my setter's bell as he returned with our first woodcock. While marveling at the mottled russet hues of its delicate feathers, I thought that if only one of these beautiful birds was the limit, I would have been satisfied. Fickle college coeds and frenetic campus life were eclipsed for a time by a reclusive little bird with a brain the size of Number 4 buckshot.

I soon learned that the season of the woodcock and the hunter pales as quickly as autumn's ephemeral blush. At best it is a brief encounter. Days shorten, frost lingers, and the chalk accompanying a flight of October woodcock soon loses its telltale whiteness to early winter snows. Though the woodcock harvest is short-lived, its sustenance nurtured my wounded anatomy and ego from season to season. Other than an occasional bow hunter, I was usually the thicket's only guest come October. During those college years of the late 1960s, the thicket's therapeutic solitude helped to shelter me from the turbulence of the times. It gave me a feeling of permanence in a social order that was rapidly changing into chaos. Its natural rhythms kept me in time with the seasons, in tune with the natural scheme of things. Within its quiet coverts I hunted woodcock and watched as the rest of the world went roaring past.

Each year since my timberdoodle baptism, I have made many pilgrimages to tortuous habitats to mingle spirits with the woodcock. Few have equaled the splendor of that first encounter, but all have been an escape to reality. Even when calmly caught in my setter's motionless stare, the woodcock's frantic flush still unnerves me. Removing thorns from my dog's pads and dabbing iodine on my own torn flesh have tempered any smugness I may have felt after taking a limit of these intriguing birds. Quantity of kill has little significance when compared with the subtle splendor of a day spent in early fall woodcock thickets. Because of the bird's capricious moods, I have come to cherish its haunts almost as much as the creature itself. I have also discovered that under certain conditions woodcock, like other upland birds, do not always hold their ground for dog and gun.

With imminent midterms cramming my brain, my third woodcock season was ushered in on the dust devils of a summerlong drought. The day was a perfect one for closing the books and testing my hunting I.Q. The thornapple thicket was parched of its perfume, and spent leaves crackled like eggshells underfoot. My setter and I tiptoed from point to point that warm October morning, with nothing escaping the covert except migrating robins and a white-tailed doe. Walking the edge of a bone-dry swampy area while my dog labored nearby in a dense stand of poplars, I heard a frantic pitter-pattering emanating from the grove and watched what appeared to be a gigantic bumblebee careen through the tussocks of marsh grass in front of me. I took two steps and a woodcock flushed in my face, frantically spiraled up behind me, then folded from an instinctive trigger pull on my sidelock. At that moment, I realized that all the birds pointed and lost that day had been half-running, half-bumbling out from under my setter's brush-cut nose. Perhaps properly bred New England woodcock do not display such a footloose tendency, but the Midwestern birds I encountered that season behaved as if

Herb Booth

they intended to create a sporting reputation all their own. I even aced my exams that semester and credit the thicket and my pointing dog for helping me to keep grade points in perspective.

Even during warm seasons I have learned that it is unwise to challenge woodcock thickets without a long-sleeved shirt and shooting glasses. Like good boots and brush pants, they are necessary shields of the pursuit. Even with this token protection, I have become enough of a stoic to accept the minor contusions and ear slaps every woodcock thicket delivers without fail. The bird is well protected by its innate ability to dance effortlessly around shrubs and trees, often leaving hunter and gun in rapt silence.

Deliberate as hunting such thickets must be, gun handling in the underbrush is more reflex action than anything else. Tutored by practical experience, I believe that a responsive, open-choked side-by-side takes to the challenge in much the same fashion as a woodcock takes to the air. Having neither the bulk of a 12 nor the toyness of a 20, the much-neglected 16-gauge double, with its efficient patterning of one-ounce field loads, is my preference for woodcock. However, for more than a century, Purdey, Holland & Holland, Boss, and other British bests have made a fairly convincing case for the lightweight 12-bore game gun. Spanish and Italian copies of these elegant double guns can also bring tears to my eyes. Whatever the choice, a high-quality, hand-built double is not so much the measure of its owner as the upland bird he hunts. As far as I am concerned, there is no more deserving gamebird in upland or lowland thickets than the North American woodcock. Worshipped with either sidelock or boxlock, this spirited bird should command the reverence of sabbath by all who are privileged to tread its hallowed ground. The more I come to respect the bird and its haunts, the more I will insist on a classic double gun to do penance in its brushy cathedrals.

Older now and far from the Ivy League campus, I often wonder if that 160-acre woodcock thicket continues to sneer at "progress." If it is still there, the masses of humanity commuting past it in cars and trains each day will likely never truly understand the plight of this diminutive wildlife oasis. For a few all-too-brief seasons that defiant thicket served up its heady spirits of the hunt to me, and I in turn shared them with my birdhunting companions. But we have talked among ourselves long enough. Many believe we have paid enough to preserve our wildlife and hunting heritage. For the sake of the woodcock and the thickets they inhabit, I will continue paying whatever it takes to enable wildlife managers to secure the breeding and migratory habitat needed to perpetuate these fascinating birds. In a country gone wildlife-stamp crazy, maybe one more to help secure the legacy of the woodcock would be a small but noble price to pay. This little bird, after all, is no less important to the overall scheme of things than those who scheme to subdue its haunts with asphalt and concrete. I didn't graduate *cum laude*, but it doesn't take a Rhodes scholar to understand that we must preserve the tenure of the woodcock if we are to pass our final exam as a species.

Each fall birdhunters witness firsthand the woodcock's dependence on healthy habitat. As stewards of its dwindling domain, we must demonstrate the wisdom of sound wildlife management to those who choose not to hunt, and encourage them to share in the responsibility of letting the woodcock fall where they may. If we do any less, the American woodcock, its thickets, and our game guns may be forever silenced, progress and higher education notwithstanding.

All-American Game Gun

When it comes to handmade double guns, I display all the objectivity of a lovesick moose. My wife, bless her understanding heart, is fortunate indeed that I do not harbor the same passion for automobiles. Our front yard would look like a used-car lot. After wining and dining an entourage of foreign and domestic 12- and 20-gauge doubles over the past three decades, I am convinced the 16-gauge side-by-side is the best choice for the uplands—although I would be hard pressed to convince all my shooting companions of this fact. It always amazes me how they can manage to limit out so frequently with their ragtag assortment of large- and small-bore shotguns. All logic aside, the 16 is as sweet as it gets. In game-gun configuration, its weight, balance, and symmetrical lines endow it with handling qualities that are second to none afield. Correctly choked and loaded, it can pattern an ounce of birdshot that will delight the most exacting master gunmaker.

America's machine age was in full flower about the time L. C. Smith No. 66898 left the Hunter Arms Company in Fulton, New York. Selling for just $32 in 1912, the 16-gauge OO Grade lacked the elegant refinement found on world-class game guns of royal pedigree. No intricate scroll or game-scene engraving adorned its graceful sidelocks. Its plainly checkered walnut lacked any flaming figure to ignite the passion that smolders deep within my gun-loving heart. Looks alone proclaimed that it was a strictly utilitarian piece of American gunmaking, and I had to have it. Though conspicuously unembellished, the lightweight sidelock was endowed with attractive lines and, more importantly, possessed the coveted handling qualities of a classic bird gun. It flaunted a functional elegance I could not resist. Reposing quietly in a distant dealer's gun room, L. C. Smith No. 66898 was about to reconfirm my faith in American game guns, few and far between as they may be.

As my beleaguered spouse and hunting companions can readily attest, if I am caught between guns come bird season I am about as contestable and pathetic as a person can get. Like dark-eyed gypsies dancing in the moonlight, many alluring 16-bores have flirted with my gunning libido over the seasons. I have lovingly handled and hunted an O-frame Parker 16 that was a joy to carry and shoot. However, as such fine and fickle doubles are wont to do, it found a new home with a hunting partner who was captivated by its hidden charms and, after weeks of lovesick supplication, paid me dearly for its affection. I recently parted with a 16-gauge Winchester Model 21 Skeet gun whose seductively tapered barrels were deadly on doves and all manner of buff-colored birds. Its beefy frame, densely grained American black walnut stock, and beavertail forearm made the attractive gun about a pound overweight for any serious affairs in the uplands. I reluctantly sold it to a dealer who had half-a-dozen suitors lined up even before the comely scattergun arrived at his shop—convincing evidence that the popularity of the 16-gauge has embraced yet another generation of birdhunters. A hand-detachable sidelock Garbi 16-bore, which shared the same fate as the O-frame Parker, also accompanied me into the field for a few seasons. Though beautifully sculpted, the Spanish smoothbore did not satisfy my desire for a classic American-built bird gun.

My feverish longing for an ever-sweeter 16 double eventually led me to a Pennsylvania purveyor of fine game guns of English, European, and American origin. The gun-wise proprietor listened patiently to my lengthy lament and said he had just received a pristine 16-gauge L. C. Smith Featherweight on consignment that might be of interest. The rare, straight-hand OO Grade lacked ejectors but seemed to have everything I wanted in a bird gun. Light and lithe, its svelte figure would surely enable me to perform with alacrity in the uplands. Tradition also dictates that a game gun with a straight grip and two locks also have two triggers to complete the classic equation. And to quash any temptation of ejecting plastic litter on the hunting grounds, an extractor gun would encourage me to carry my empty shell casings home. In a moment of weakness, I told the old gunnie to turn away all takers and made the necessary arrangements to put the vintage Smith in my gun cabinet. Not wanting to alter the gun's original $2\,^9/_{16}$-inch chambers, I also ordered a case of 2½-inch, 2½-dram, one-ounce game loads in Number 8 shot—plenty of punch for quail, woodcock, and early grouse.

When L. C. Smith No. 66898 arrived, its delicately hand-filed frame and smoothly struck barrels gave an immediate impression of quality. The breech flowed seamless into the fences, and the top lever was still a few generations right of center. After admiring the tight little gun for a few days, I composed a list of modifications that would make the octogenarian double fit my taste and physique. The 28-inch tubes were choked tighter than necessary for upland work, and the bottom of the right barrel had a very small dent about halfway up. Without hesitation I sent the barrels to a masterful father-and-son team in New York who opened them up to Skeet 1 and Skeet 2. My field experience has shown that such a choke combination can cope with most upland shooting contingencies. By inserting a metal plug of the proper diameter down the bore, the barrel men also removed and stress-relieved the small dent in the right barrel. They polished the bores mirror bright and pronounced them ready for another lifetime or two of service. For three generations this New York family has been expertly servicing and restoring Parkers and other fine American doubles. Their dedication to America's gunmaking tradition keeps the hope alive in my heart.

Except for a couple of tortured screw heads—a cruel fate imposed on many an old double by mindless gun hacks—the Featherweight Smith's metal-to-metal fit and function were flawless. However, no matter how mechanically perfect or well finished a game gun may be, I have no use for it unless I can make peace with its stock. Length of pull on the pre-1913 Smith measured just 13⅞ inches, and the drop at comb and heel were excessive for me. The dimensions may have suited someone of average build, but to fit my tall frame, a new stock would have to be built for the gun. Since many of the older L. C. Smiths were originally stocked with tight-grained English walnut, I decided to restock the vintage double with that same fine wood.

There are still a good number of L. C. Smiths, Parkers, Foxes, Lefevers, and Ithacas with fluid-steel barrels that remain in excellent condition but are difficult to shoot because of hind-leg stock dimensions and tightly choked bores. Restocked to fit their owners and rebored for the uplands, these wonderful old side-by-sides can still offer years of faithful service without breaking the bank. Some of the old Damascus-barreled guns can also be sleeved with new steel tubes to handle modern ammunition. And to preserve an old double's collectibility, the original stock can be retained for future trade or sale. The more I come to appreciate high-quality wingshooting experiences, the more convinced I am in the logic of choosing a pristine American classic double as a hunting companion.

Sometimes locating the right piece of walnut for a restocking job can be a frustrating ordeal. Fortunately, my search for the perfect buttstock required only one phone call. An old friend and high-plains gunmaker rummaged through his well-seasoned cache of English walnut blanks and sent me a figure-filled buttstock that would snuggle up nicely to the Smith's frame and sidelocks. As it must to help prevent cracking around the inletting, the grain at the head of the stock blank ran straight and unblemished. In a world increasingly dominated by plastics and laminates, connoisseurs of fine stock wood are getting harder to find. My friend and his wood are treasures indeed.

Though driver's license, checking account, and other numbers may escape me, I can recite my stock dimensions without hesitation. They are:

Length of Pull: 15½ inches
Drop at Comb: 1³/₈ inches
Drop at Heel: 2¹/₈ inches
Cast-On: ¹/₈ inch
Pitch: 0 inches

With my port-side master eye, the Cast-On measurement indicates that I shoot from the left shoulder—no small task, considering that I do everything else right-handed.

Much like the beleaguered golfer sorting out club length and swing weight, I arrived at my stock measurements through years of trial and error and a couple of try-gun fittings by some very knowledgeable shooting instructors. I firmly believe every shotgunner who is serious about birdhunting and sporting clays should schedule at least one try-gun fitting with a reputable instructor. I was fortunate to meet such an individual a few years back. The affable gentleman has been stocking shotguns for nearly forty years and can render personal stock measurements that can perform magic on feathered and clay targets alike. I told him of my hopeless bird-gun obsession and asked him to restock the 16-gauge Smith. At the time, I was unaware of his lifelong love affair with the L. C. Smith hammerless shotgun, and spent many a long hour admiring and fondling his fine collection. He even maintains a storage bin full of original L. C. Smith parts to help rekindle the romance in a cherished old Smith.

When I finally arrived at the stockmaker's bustling shop, he gave me a tour of his well-organized eight-man operation. From workbenches festooned with hand tools of the stockmaker's trade to fine-tuned stock-duplicating machinery, the entire shop was reminiscent of a golden age when craftsmanship, not inflated corporate profits, was the compelling force behind the gun. The pungent aroma of fresh-cut and sanded walnut permeated the establishment, scenting every breath I took.

My stockmaker was impressed with the well-figured English walnut blank I provided him. After wetting the buttstock to study its color and grain flow, he sorted through a large rack of fore-end blanks and selected the perfect color match. Although borderless checkering seems to be the current benchmark, I requested that he re-create the Smith's original checkering pattern on the straight grip and forearm. And to further assuage my purist tendencies, he agreed that a hand-rubbed oil finish would complement the high-grade walnut very nicely. Displaying more than skin-deep beauty, an oil finish also enables me to treat the minor scratches and contusions that await every bird gun in the puckerbrush and tag alders. To give the double a subtle, yet distinctive touch of class, I also requested that an ebony fore-end tip be added and that the plastic buttplate be discarded in favor of a checkered butt. Such subtle refinements have a way of comforting birdhunters when the hair suddenly grays and the seasons roll too swiftly past. As L. C. Smith so proudly proclaimed in its advertising material, "A thing of beauty is a joy forever."

My woodworking friend assured me he could match my dimensions without bending the Smith's

action tangs. He went on to explain the techniques and tools he would use to restock the sidelock. Wood selection and preparation, he explained, are essential. Most gunstock blanks are sawn into three-inch-thick slabs from the root and crotch portions of mature walnut trees, and graded according to figure. Good wood blanks range in price from $250 to more than $1,000. Most stock blanks spend at least six months kiln-drying to attain the proper moisture content. When the moisture meter registers between 6 and 12 percent, the walnut is considered stable for stock work. However, truly fine walnut blanks have their end grain sealed with pitch or paraffin and are aged for years in a climate-controlled environment. Careful seasoning increases the stability and workability of fine walnut. Each blank is closely examined to determine grain structure, flaws, and figure. Sapwood portions of the blank, if present, are usually avoided. A pre-cut template is often used to trace the desired stock profile on the blank. On an older gun like my Smith, the original stock is covered from comb to heel with masking tape and then layered with plastic body putty to build up the required drop dimensions. Using the built-up stock as a master, an inletting cut is made on the stock blank with a one-off duplicating machine to roughly accommodate the frame and sidelocks. The plastic putty and masking tape are then removed from the original stock. With the roughed-out blank held firmly in the stockmaker's cork-lined vise, the top tang of the action is inletted, with care being taken to ensure that the sideplates are in proper alignment. To snug the action up to the stock, a hole with wood pull is drilled through the top tang. The bottom tang (trigger guard) receives the same treatment.

Unfortunately, L. C. Smiths have a nasty habit of cracking around the sidelocks. Proper wood choice and precisely chamfered inletting at the head of the stock and chamfering cuts around the lockplates help eliminate this malady, as does some preventive maintenance. My friend emphasized that tang-screw tension should be checked periodically on all L. C. Smiths (and other older doubles) to prevent recoil from damaging a loosened stock. Oil-soaked wood at the head of the stock is another culprit that can lead to future inletting headaches. Eccentric as it may seem, I stand my double guns upside down in the gun cabinet to prevent any excess lubricating oil from invading the jaws of the stock.

Making the wood appear as if it has grown around the metal is the goal of all custom stockers. Such inletting requires painstaking fitting and refitting. To highlight contact points, a fine film of inletting black is brushed on all metal surfaces cradled in the jaws of the stock. Many traditional English gunmakers still smoke the metal with lampblack to achieve the desired wood-to-metal fit. With the use of various chisels, blackened wood is gradually removed where a wedging or tapering fit is prescribed. In other areas, such as bearing points, little if any wood is removed.

Because drop and cast dimensions are crucial to final fit, initial stock shaping is done with the bar-rels on the action. All shaping and contouring is done around a center line that is penciled on top of the stock from head to butt. This center line ensures a symmetrically fit action and enables the stockmaker to check and recheck all drop and cast dimensions.

Once the desired stock measurements have been captured, the wood surface is prepared to receive the oil finish. The stock is hand-sanded and wetted and sanded again, using ever-finer grits of sandpaper, until the wood surface is marble-smooth. A good hand-rubbed oil finish begins with ten to twelve coats of pure linseed oil, which can be mixed with alkanet root and other natural ingredients to produce the desired color and absorption. In the old gun trade here and abroad, these oil-based concoctions were often passed from father to son for generations. Unfortunately, like case-hardening secrets, many of these oil formulas were not written down, and were often carried to the grave. I wish I could have been privy to some of this information before it passed into oblivion. During the finishing process, excess stock oil is wiped off between applications, and after every three coats or so the walnut is lightly sanded with 600-grit sandpaper. Unlike varnish or synthetics that merely coat the surface, hand-rubbed oil produces a durable, warm finish that is actually part of the wood.

As appealing as well-executed engraving, fine stock checkering requires an experienced hand and a keen eye. I requested that the wood on the Smith be checkered twenty-four lines to the inch. Delicate but still functional, the neatly pointed diamonds would help me keep a good grip on the gun. A checkering template is used to draw the pattern outline on the grip and fore arm. Guiding lines are then drawn in pencil every half-inch or inch within the borders to maintain parallel checkering cuts through the grip contours. Razor-sharp checkering tools are used to achieve a consistent cutting depth and uniformly shaped diamonds. To help gain more purchase on the shoulder, the butt of my Smith was checkered with elongated diamonds twenty lines to the inch. If needed, a small core is cut in the end of the buttstock to add or remove weight for proper gun balance.

After a long summer's wait, I was anxious to field-test the restocked Smith in September dove fields. My friendly master in wood called early in the fall and said I had better come get the pretty little gun before he could figure out a way to talk me out of it. With its new, fully figured cellulose, the L. C. Smith is indeed a fetching little game gun. Its fit and feel are excellent and should help eliminate most of my pitiful excuses for hustling feathered targets unscathed through the woods. Such craftsmanship does take time, and under normal circumstances a good stockmaker can restock a double gun in about four to six months, depending on desired options and his work load. Sidelocks, of course, require more time and attention than boxlocks.

As the turn of another century approaches, it gratifies me to know that America is still home to so many talented craftsmen. Nearly a hundred years ago, similar proud American workers built some of the most innovative and reliable double guns ever made. This enviable tradition lives on in the dedicated individuals who have given new life to a sweet old L. C. Smith double gun. Restocked in handsome English walnut, L. C. Smith No. 66898 is truly "a thing of beauty" and will no doubt be "a joy forever," or at least until some other enchanted bird gun or envious hunting companion beckons me to forsake my vows of fidelity.

At long last, my perennial quest for the perfect Yankee double has been sated. The Smith's elegantly struck 28-inch barrels, splinter fore-arm, graceful lockplates, Featherweight frame, twin triggers, straight grip, and tailored stock combine to make this six-pound 16-gauge an all-American game gun. Now, if I can just conjure up the perfect bird dog, bird cover, and bird load, my autumnal afflictions will be cured and my sainted wife and bemused hunting partners will find peace at long last.

Grouse Country

Each year there seems to be a little less of what we all need more of—grouse country. To some, it may be no more than a secluded place where windblown pines chase the road noise away. For others, it may be a labyrinth of unkempt logging roads longing to be explored with backpacks or cross-country skis. Most look upon such country as little more than a visual tranquilizer as they travel on the interstate. To me it is all of these things and more. It is a close-knit community where deer flash white flags at clumsy intruders; where raptors soar above the treetops and rodents scramble through pungent debris on the forest floor; where crystalline brooks carry an occasional woodcock feather and the prospect of speckled trout frying over a campfire. All of these visions are kept simmering in the skillet of my memory between hunting seasons. Though I may seek to grasp the rhyme and reason of grouse country, it is the random hand of nature that provides haven for both the pursued and the pursuer.

What is modern civilization to make of the ruffed grouse's society? With my passion for the forested hills and a primordial desire to immerse my soul in second-growth, I need strong doses of grouse country. The hunter, as he has for thousands of years, reigns as ultimate keeper of the grouse's domain. Our concern and our dollars provide for the pine forest, the aspen groves, the hardwood mix, and the habitat management so essential to this gallant bird's long-term survival. As the growing world imposes its far-reaching impact on the environment, the ruffed grouse owes its very existence to those of us who hunt it. We in turn must remain vigilant in our efforts to conserve grouse habitat on public and private land. To me a woodland without grouse is like a life without spirit. These gamebirds symbolize all that is wild in America. Grouse and grouse country are God's potion for those of us who must escape to reality each fall. Lost souls find themselves in the grouse woods. It is an enchanted kingdom where game, gun, and hunter become one. The sleek side-by-side I carry into grouse country each season is a means to celebrate the ruffed grouse's society, not an end.

With my double broken open and cradled over my arm, I watched my setter amble down the sandy logging road in a sustained gait that told me he still had a couple of hours of hunting left in him. For most of an unseasonably warm October morning we had roamed Wisconsin's rugged hill country without moving a bird. Stalking through second-growth pines and tangled grapevines, we explored all the classic cover types in search of grouse. The short-order cook at the diner where I stopped for a predawn breakfast said the birds were on a down cycle and I would be hard-pressed to pop a cap. The cook's prophecy was shattered by an avian explosion a yard deep off the logging road. Instinctively, I raised my double and watched my tandem loads of chilled Number 8 shot slip from their chambers and fall harmlessly to my feet. The grouse roared through the trees and was gone in an instant. Both amused and disappointed, I barely caught my setter's backward glance as he broke off his point before continuing down the logging road. First the bird, now my dog. How much humbling can a grown man take?

After slowly strolling through a vaulted cathedral of color-washed hardwoods, I came to a rickety wooden bridge that crossed a shimmering spring creek. I found my dog reposing sphinx-like in the middle of the shallow brook lapping up the cool water. The rivulet was too inviting to pass up. I gingerly set my side-by-side on the fern-blanketed bank and slid down to the spring in time to see a woodcock flush a few yards from where my shotgun reposed. My dog and I watched the bird's batlike shenanigans until it disappeared downstream over a wall of jack pines. Brook trout darted wildly under the bridge as I knelt to take a drink. My dog sloshed by and shook his burden of water over most of my backside. Such are the joys and rewards of a devout grouse hunter.

I was prepared for the second grouse that flushed later that morning. My dog bumped it from a crowded stand of aspen, and after some indiscriminate pruning of foliage with my right barrel, I brought the large drummer solidly to earth with my left. I perceived a contented look in my dog's eyes as he proudly delivered the grouse to my outstretched hand. It was a mature bird with a tailfeather spread whose splendor could have competed with a chieftain's headdress. The bird was too handsome and hard won to be stuffed unceremoniously into my game bag, so I spent a long time admiring and preening its plumage, then clutched its feet and hand-carried it out of the fragrant forest that had given it, my dog, and me life.

As I walked along the eroded macadam toward the distant truck, with my setter straining at his lead, I thought about that venerable fraternity of birdhunters who have strived to dignify the grouse with pen and ink. Try as they might to enlighten a hunter's heart as he draws on his aromatic briar and pets his tired gun dog in front of a crackling hearth, there is really no substitute for a trek through grouse country in the fall. Perhaps it is a little like trying to describe the aroma of wood smoke on a frosty evening, or the smell of hickory-smoked bacon sizzling over a campfire, or the bite of fresh-brewed sassafras tea after a long day of chasing snowshoe hares through the tamaracks, or the sensuous smell of a freshly spent paper shotgun shell, or the high-up sound of geese singing their way south. Such experiences lose something when translated into mere words. Granted, I can find few greater pleasures in the dead of winter than rekindling days afield with a good book by one of the old masters on the art and science of "partridge" hunting. But the hunt itself transcends any vicarious significance writers might attach to the experience.

A devoted grouse hunter, I am as concerned as much about the grouse's environment as the bird itself. Crimson sumac, bleached and bare aspen, netted grapevines, flaming maples, verdant ferns, and towering pines—all are woven into the many-splendored fabric that blankets grouse country. I realized long ago that if I was to survive for very long in the thick grouse woods, I would have to become an incurable romantic. Pragmatic individuals quickly conclude that grouse are impossible to hunt, let alone hit, especially with a gun that must be correctly mounted, pointed, and fired within a second or so.

Most grouse hunters I have encountered are rare birds indeed, and their grouse guns usually assume the character of their keepers. From frail and spindly 28-bore sidelocks to long-barreled 12-repeaters, each gun must quickly adapt to the frantic response of hunter to bird or die on the rack. I am dead sure that the perfect grouse gun, like the perfect wingshot, has yet to be created. If it has, it remains a well-kept secret. However, the banter of my expert companions circled 'round a hissing pot-bellied stove in the dead of winter could lead me to believe otherwise. David is convinced his treasured Fox 20-bore is the best gun ever made for grouse, quail, woodcock, or any other bird that causes dogs to freeze in their tracks. Luke, on the other hand, wields a 12-gauge Model 12 for everything that flies. Uncle John and Frank, both of whom are less inclined to obsessive gun behavior, will kill birds with just about anything that shoots. Mark, ever the handler, thinks we should all consider dogs more and guns less.

Before the tamaracks yellow and the maples turn crimson, I have usually been fortunate enough to keep at least one gun that fits or, God forbid, groove my tortured anatomy to fit the gun. Either way, a dead grouse is a dead grouse, and the choice of a sporting piece for the purpose is as personal as one's preference for the fairer sex—although, much to my chagrin, the latter often requires considerably more care and feeding. All my birdhunting friends agree that a well-fit, well-balanced game gun compensates for reflexes dulled by a day of trudging the rugged hill country that grouse usually prefer. Add to this gun a slim, straight grip, double triggers, and splinter fore-end, and you come about as close to an ideal grousing instrument as the Lord will allow, at least to my way of thinking. And since our Maker saw fit to position my eyes alongside one another, I am inclined to endorse the same arrangement when it comes to barrels on a double gun.

My pet grouse gun is six pounds of unadorned steel and well-figured English walnut built with hard-boiled Yankee ingenuity just about the time the *Titanic* took on a fresh load of ice. Over-and-unders seem to be the rage now, and I can understand why, given their compelling design and improved handling qualities. But for me, vertical barrels just don't seem to nestle as comfortably into the crook of the arm or over the shoulder as side-by-side barrels do. Nor do they symbolize as well the rich birdhunting tradition Americans have enjoyed for well over a century. The side-by-side game gun is as natural a response to shooting grouse on the wing as hunting instincts are to a man. Perhaps technology will evolve to the point where a laser gun or some such contrivance will antiquate the classic double gun, but I'll never insult a grouse with one.

As the demands of progress diminish and degrade the hunting grounds, I suppose it is inevitable that the day will eventually come when those of us who cherish wild birds and a limited kill will retire our smoothbores rather than capitulate to the put-and-take preserves that most hunters will have to patronize. Through public scientific wildlife management and a comprehensive private land ethic, measures can still be taken to conserve the ruffed grouse's wild domain. Hunters, as usual, must lead the way.

As in times past, there remains a great deal of difference between hunting and shooting. It is a distinction that separates those who like to keep score from those who do not, from those who prefer a deeply personal experience and those who take pride in public exhibition. Grouse thrive on solitude. I believe it is the solitary hunter and dog who are the unheralded champions in the grouse's pine-scented arena, anonymous as the game they give fair chase to. I suppose it

Herb Booth

is purism of sorts to demand that a man hunt wild birds or none at all. But such is what enticed us from the caves out into the wilderness eons ago. As sad as it sounds, we may have civilized ourselves to the extent where hunting will soon become but a brief footnote in a history book, and no longer a primordial passion for the game. I learned early on that I must first lose myself in wilderness before I could find real purpose for my sporting life. Grouse country tempts me from secure surroundings and casts its enchanted spell on all my companions who have the courage to get lost amid the forested hills and secluded valleys.

After sucking the last bit of flavor from a hollow grouse bone, I am further convinced these great birds were created especially for birdhunters. A ruffed grouse gives its life fully to the birdhunter who knows how to enjoy the woods and wood smoke. Because of this bird, I have spent a small fortune to build a shotgun that honors the ritual. Every time I look down its gracefully tapered tubes, or rub oil into its deeply figured walnut, or admire its elegant symmetry, I am really paying homage to America's rich grouse-hunting heritage. The gun and the grouse will pass through my life. They will enrich it and be passed along to another generation of hunters who will, I hope, nurture the same sentiment. I see the graying muzzle of my setter, contemplate the gray hair around my own temples, and know why God created the grouse. It is His promise that "to everything there is a season and a purpose under heaven." As David would often say on our seasonal sojourns to the northwoods, "Thank God for grouse country."

Smitty

My bird gun was hurting. It was a beautiful old VH Parker O-frame built prior to World War I. The hand-worn side-by-side was beginning to show its age. Its spring-tension fore-end was starting to dance around on the barrels, and I didn't know how much longer it was going to hold the gun together. Still naive to the ways of the world, I took the gun to a local "gunsmith" who boasted he would have the "little jewel" fixed in a week or two. After I made several futile attempts to reach him, he called six months later to say that he had tried everything to repair the fore-end. He told me the gun was worn-out and should be retired as a wallhanger. I took the gun home and discovered that he had indeed "tried everything" to repair it. Every screwhead on the gun was out of registration and marred from his clumsy incompetence. Among other things, the barrel hook had been peened out of shape in a futile attempt to draw the fore-end up tight.

After a great deal of searching, I located an irascible old "smitty" who worked out of his basement. The cramped hole was cluttered with dusty tool-and-die equipment, coffee cans, and Mason jars full of miscellaneous parts. Firearms with repair tags filled every nook and cranny around his oil-stained workbench.

"Who sent ya?" he growled. I told him that I had found his name listed in an old *Gun Digest* and that I had about given up finding a gunsmith who could bring my double back to life. I asked him if he could repair the gun.

"Maybe I can, maybe I can't," was his terse reply. "All depends on how I feel and how much I'm willing to put up with your long hair and dumb questions." To say that the man was opinionated and somewhat right-wing would be an understatement. A week later he called and told me to come get my gun out of his basement. Not a trace of the previous "gunsmith's" butchering was evident, and the old double was as solid and tight as the day it had left the factory. The parts and screws he couldn't find in his eclectic inventory, he made by hand. From that day forward I called him Mr. Wizard, he dubbed me the mad Russian, and we shared each other's passion for fine guns until the car accident that had confined him to his basement gun shop finally claimed his life.

The next time I visited his cluttered hideaway, I brought him a Civil-War-vintage percussion double shotgun that Uncle John inherited from his great-grandfather. The wrist of its straight-hand stock was split open, and slivers of wood reached outward like a gnarled rootwad.

"Jesus, boy!" he recoiled. "Wha'dja do, buttstroke a charging rogue cockbird with this old smokepole?" I told him the muzzleloader had sentimental value and I was restoring it for a friend of the family.

"Well, why didn't ya say so to begin with?" he barked. "I'll see what I can do. Oh, by the way," he added, "you wouldn't know anyone who might be interested in an old Parker double, would ya?" He nonchalantly reached around his bench and handed me a BHE 12-gauge that sent a chill through me like a nor'easter.

"I've seen this gun before," I said. "Where'd you get it?" He told me about a portly traveling salesman who used to stop by the shop periodically during swings through his territory.

"I repaired its cussed ejectors," Smitty growled, "and the silver-tongued S.O.B. has never returned for the gun. It's been over three years now. Tried callin' him a few years back, but his phone's disconnected. Wish I had a dollar for every shootin' iron that's been left down here. Looks like the police association will have another item for their fund-raiser this year."

I stared incredulously at the elegant double, fondled it for a short eternity, then handed it back, without saying a word.

"What's the matter, sonny?" he snipped. "Too much gun for ya?" I couldn't bring myself to tell him that the gun had already stolen my heart once a long time ago, and the second time was certainly a charm. As Smitty predicted, the pristine BHE did indeed wind up in the police auction later that fall. I was off hunting grouse in the northwoods and wasn't there to watch the physician who made the high bid.

Less than a month after that visit, Mr. Wizard phoned and said, "Your World War II canoe paddle's ready!" When I claimed the antique double, I accused the old curmudgeon of completely restocking the piece. I closely examined every inch of the repair and couldn't find so much as a blemish in the slim-wristed stock.

"Now, don't you and your friend go rowing any boats with this blunderbuss," he said, gently stroking the buttstock. "I wouldn't think twice about shootin' it, though. It's a right smart bit of English gunmaking. By the way, do you think old Joe Manton ever got a chance to 'field-test' any of his guns?"

Sensitive to his deteriorating physical condition and confinement, I told him with all the sincerity I could muster that all the great old gunnies were probably just like him, slaves to the bench. His eyes brightened with my simple summation. He straightened up in his wheelchair and told me to tell some of my friends to drop by every now and then to talk guns. "Wouldn't mind puttin' up with their dumb questions, either," he offered. I told him he didn't know what he was letting himself in for, that all my friends were incorrigible ear-benders. I also told him not to blame me if they ever wasted his time or cluttered up his shop with their unclaimed guns.

Anyone who owns a high-grade Parker, Fox, L. C. Smith, Lefever, Model 21 Winchester, or Ithaca knows the anguish of entrusting his prized possession to an unfamiliar gunsmith. It's difficult for me to imagine the owner of a Purdey, Holland, Francotte, or other fine European double ever wanting to tempt the transatlantic gremlins or play paper chase with customs officials every time his alter ego hiccups. A good gunsmith like Smitty is a godsend.

I once asked a master gunmaker from Birmingham, England, for his thoughts on gun repair. First off, he told me there was a great deal of difference between a gunsmith and a gunmaker. "With most mass-produced shotguns like pumps and autoloaders," he said in his lilting English accent, "you can still order replacement parts from the manufacturer, but a handmade double gun is a different cup of tea entirely." He went on to say that because best-grade

doubles are built by hand one at a time, interchange-
able parts are virtually nonexistent. Consequently,
a gunsmith of best guns must be a consummate craftsman. He must be part metallurgist, well-versed in
annealing, tempering, and case-hardening alloyed
steel; and part stockmaker, adept at inletting, checkering, repairing, and finishing various types of
American and English walnut. More than just a jack-
of-all-trades, he must become a master gun builder
before hanging out his shingle.

Maybe it is the nature of the profession, but
every gunsmith I ever met who was worth his bluing
salt has been a real character. To hear them talk,
they can truly fix anything afflicting guns. Numbed
by long-winded dissertations on some esoteric phase

of gunsmithing or the deplorable state of politics and the nation, I have learned to carefully target my questions during my frequent visits to the "Smitty" or suffer the consequences.

Once, I made the mistake of asking Mr. Wizard if he thought chamber-forcing cone tapers had any real impact on shotgun patterns. "Jesus, Joseph, and Mary, sonny!" he wailed. "I thought you knew something about shotguns! Just one dumb question after another," he said, slowly shaking his head. He leaned back in his chair, his eyes glazing over with didactic resolve, and began his lecture:

"You see, boy, a shot charge is like a mouthful of food. If you force down too big a bite through a throat that's too small, it's gonna hurt on its slow slide to your stomach. No doubt some indigestion's gonna creep back up later on. Now, if you was to eat a civilized portion instead of cramming your mouth full, you could swallow and digest it without much trouble."

"Oh!" I responded. "You mean like always using 3-inch shells in 20-gauge guns?"

"Exactly!" he shot back, his voice gathering volume and velocity. "Ten pounds of crap in a five-pound bag that can kick like a Missouri mule and cause some nasty chamber pressures. But just let me stretch them cones out a bit, add a touch of back-boring, and it would smooth out the recoil some and give the shot column an easier ride down the barrel. Still following me, sonny? It's called bore scrub, boy, and even with all these newfangled shot cups and choke tubes, it can play hell with your patterns. Every shotgun and every load's different. You got to play with them some to get what you want."

"Kinda like courting a lady," I responded.

"Now you're getting the idea, sonny!" he gleamed. "A few thousandths here, a few thousandths there, and pretty soon she's printin' out patterns as pretty as you please."

Two hours later he slowed his chant, came out of his trance, and gave me hell for wasting his whole afternoon. I didn't ask him too many open-ended questions after that, especially dumb ones.

Of course, I and my wingshooting friends are a similarly passive lot of characters, seldom entertaining contrary opinions about bird guns or beautiful women. Why Smitty furrows his brow and turns a deaf ear every time I begin soapboxing the 16-gauge as the best all-round bird gun and Marilyn Monroe as the all-time sex goddess is a real mystery to me. The man has either shot away his hearing or has lost all objectivity. What a character.

Best Bird Guns

It beckoned to me like a seductive siren on some midnight sea. I had heard the song before, but on workman's wages I still couldn't afford to dance to it. The temptress of my dreams this time was a beautiful round-action Boss 12-bore sidelock, a classic "best gun" from the British Isles. I knew the thick-skinned gun dealer wouldn't accept my pathetic attempts to woo him down on price, so I lusted quietly over the side-by-side for a few precious minutes before reluctantly placing it back in the rack with others of its kind.

The passage of time has not diminished my desire for that gorgeous game gun. Its understated elegance, precise fit, and lively feel linger with me still.

I suppose every serious birdhunter entertains a fantasy or two about a best gun he would like to possess, or more accurately, be possessed by. In typical English fashion, the term "best gun" was coined by London's master gun builders more than a century ago. Such prestigious makers as Manton, Lancaster, Purdey, Churchill, and Westley Richards fashioned state-of-the-art doubles that were truly the best of their kind in the world—bespoke guns, custom built for their owners.

But what is a best gun—really. As related earlier, when I was a lad of 11 my best gun was a crude Winchester Model 37 single-shot that helped seal my addiction to wingshooting. It was the only gun I owned. The small bore, though highly revered by me, was mostly machine made and, by English standards, had all the handling characteristics of a crowbar. However, I did manage to pry enough birds down from the autumn skies to appease my developing male ego and provide a few meager meals at home.

Somewhere between then and now, a smoothbore connoisseur was created. I really don't know how it happened, any more than I remember what I did right when I shot my first quail on the wing. All I know is that I now have enough gun books to rival the Library of Congress, and my acquired taste in game guns could bankrupt Fort Knox.

My evolution as a birdhunter and shotgun devotee progressed along the natural path from quantity to quality until nothing less than a properly pointed wild bird, taken with a classic side-by-side, could warm my sporting blood.

A small flame began to smolder in me when a longtime Kiwi acquaintance dropped by to show off a recently acquired matched pair of Stephen Grant game guns. After handling the new doubles and inspecting their superlative workmanship, I was tempted to liquidate my motley assortment of Parkers, Smiths, and 21s for just one of the elegant Grants.

"Go ahead, mate," my jovial friend invited. "Put it to your shoulder and snap the locks." Both tumblers fell swiftly and crisply on the snap caps. When

I opened the gun, I was amazed by the precision of the action, the authoritative kick of the ejectors, and the fit and feel of the stock. Even more impressive, though, was the realization that both guns had been fabricated with simple tools primarily by hand. My friend rekindled a fire that was ignited nearly four decades ago when I stared covetously through a window at a BHE Parker displayed on waves of royal blue velvet.

Just as I have come to cherish every moment afield, whether or not I take a limit of birds, my passion is once again ablaze with the desire to distill all my guns into one best gun. It's a natural evolution, I guess. With age comes discernment. With experience comes the wise pursuit of simplicity. A best gun symbolizes all that is right about wingshooting. It simplifies form and function; it defines quality and performance. At the age now where I have nothing to prove to myself or my hunting companions, I would just as soon hit or miss a rocketing grouse or speeding quail with a best gun and know that I gave my upland life the best I had to give. Birdhunting, after all, is not a competitive sport. It is a blissful quest for self-perfection. A perfect gun, a perfect dog, a perfect day afield. Perfection. A best gun is as close to it as I will ever come.

"Don't worry, mate," my down-under friend promised as he closed and strapped the oak-and-leather case around the Grants. "If I ever sell them, I'll give you first crack." Just as perfection haunts the master gunmaker, I have a perennial obsession for those rare fall days when the mystical is transformed into reality by a field-champion point, a textbook shot, or a brace or two of wild birds. "It's a bugger of a book you're writin', mate," my fine friend comments while lowering the Grants into the cavernous trunk of his Continental. "Don't forget to pen me into it. Maybe I'll write you into my will for the guns."

I still hear from him every now and then on his return trips from exotic destinations. Our single passion for twin tubes always dominates our conversations. In loving detail he tells me about his new acquisitions—a keenly engraved Cogswell and Harrison coerced from an ignorant wog, an immaculate Purdey taken in trade for a fortune in split-cane rods and a bundle of cash, a W. & C. Scott 20-bore liberated below fair market value from a widow's deceased husband's vaulted collection. I treasure each and every one of his conquests, as I do the humble

Smith O-Grade I find myself carrying more and more into the game fields. Plain though it is, it's my best gun when I point it right. My friend knows I'll always be in awe of his English bests. I know he'll always have one more gun than he can shoot. Together we appreciate all that is right about fine double guns. We are "best" friends. Someday I'll befriend a setter with the same taste for birds and autumn-tinted game fields. When I do, I'll take another step closer to perfection. On a resplendent October day, he'll point a grouse in the crimson woods and I'll swing through it with my best form and function. He'll retrieve the bird, and I will be in awe of him. On that day in the woods, he'll point me the way to blissful perfection.

Fine bird guns and bird dogs will always be a passion with me, one my patient wife hopes someday I will outgrow. She often hears me reverently mumbling names like Lang, Bonehill, Atkin, Boswell, Beesley, Baker, Smith, Parker, Lefever, Fox, and the like as I grope through towering stacks of books to flush out some overlooked fact of the gunmakers' art. During these frequent seizures, my doting children see the blank stare in my eyes and know their impertinent questions will go unanswered. They know, too, that their father will be lost in mindless bliss until their mother raises her voice and lowers the boom.

Gone forever are those simple adolescent days when a hunting boy's heart could be won with a hardware-store hammer gun. Finely stocked and engraved sidelock doubles are now the object of my unfaltering affection, not because of the snobbery they often evoke, or even that their value as investments continues to escalate, but simply because they are the ultimate expression of the gunmaker's craft—which has been refined in game fields and workshops worldwide for over two hundred years.

Whether we Yanks like it or not, the Brits perfected the classic game gun design more than a century ago. The only real improvements to its form and function have been the introduction of modern manufacturing techniques and stronger steel alloys. But now, as then, the final fit and finish of a best bird gun is still dependent on the knowing eyes and skilled hands of the master gunmaker. While the world races headlong into high-tech oblivion, there are still a few gifted stalwarts who work long hours to keep the proud gunmaking tradition alive. They are the rare men who can transform raw wood and forged steel into shooting instruments of the finest precision; who can fit a shotgun to the physical nuances and personal tastes of the most finicky wingshooter; who can bore a choke that will pattern birdshot consistently, whether close-in among the tag alders or far out over the rolling broomsedge or fragrant heather. They are a rare breed indeed, and the product of their labor is to be coveted and enjoyed by discriminating birdhunters worldwide.

As my Kiwi friend has made me painfully aware, the cost of such painstaking craftsmanship can be princely. Copious man-hours are spent shaping metal, contouring wood, filing and fitting parts, and embellishing surfaces before a best gun can wear its badge of excellence. On average, some 750 hours of intense labor are lavished on an English, Italian, Belgian, French, German, or Spanish best-grade double shotgun. It's not unusual to wait two or three years for a dream gun to be completed. Before all is said and done, best guns can trim the budget by $5,000 to

$60,000 or more, depending on maker and options selected. But for a lifetime of faithful service, a best gun, properly tended, will oblige like no other, increasing the quality of experiences afield with each passing season. The trouble with most American consumers today, it has been said, is that they know the cost of everything and the value of nothing. Considering the cost of an average automobile, which depreciates immediately after purchase, the logic of a best bird gun becomes even more apparent as its value appreciates through the years. My darling wife, unfortunately, remains unconvinced of this truism, which may also explain why I'm still driving a 1978 Detroit chariot.

However, best status is not reserved just for English and European double guns. Most of the higher-grade American Model 21s, Parkers, Smiths, Foxes, Lefevers, Ithacas, and Pachmayr upgrades exhibit the same high degree of craftsmanship as their overseas counterparts. On the collectors' circuit, many of these grand old Yankee classics are commanding five-figure sums, especially in the smaller gauges. A few original Parker A-1 Special 28-bores have reached six digits.

But just what does all of this high-roller best-gun talk have to do with the wingshooter who is often hard-pressed to pay for his kid's braces? Like fine art, which can be appreciated without being owned, a best gun combines artistry with utility to epitomize our great sporting heritage. And who knows, maybe someday I will discover one of these treasures hidden away in a rich uncle's attic, or receive a windfall to make the investment of a lifetime. Until then, it's comforting to know that misery loves company, and I am not the only love-struck game gunner pining away for some costly vision of finely shaped wood and steel.

Unfortunately, each year, fewer and fewer of the gunmasters hang out their shingles. Those who remain in the trade are treasures above and beyond the cold bottom line of Wall Street economics. Though England remains the progenitor of the classic sidelock game gun, France, Spain, Italy, and other European countries have all had their moments in the sun, and some continue to hold on in spite of a changing world.

With my champagne taste and beer budget, the staggering cost of a best bird gun still causes me deep pangs of despair, if not disbelief. But as my lovely wife always says, whenever I am overcome with longing for such a gun, "Where there's a will, there's a won't!" She's right, of course, but somehow, some way, someday when my lost and battered ship comes limping in, I will own a best bird gun. And if, by some miracle of fate, a wealthy friend remembers me in a will, there'll most certainly be a way. Besides, if you are a hopeless romantic like me, how can you put a price tag on sheer wingshooting bliss, perfect wife excluded?

Gray Ghosts

The sprawling sheep pasture shimmered under the hot September sun. Off in the hazy distance, an abandoned railroad bed concealed three young hunters who were keeping sharp lookout on the high-tension lines that dissected the rolling pastureland. Every so often a wisp of gray would alight on one of the sagging wires, sit stoically for a while, then flutter down to glean weed seeds in the pasture below.

"It's your turn, Frank," whispered one of the hunters. "Keep low, and don't forget to take the safety off this time." Stealth was at work in the wind-blown pasture. Frank clutched a battered old Stevens bolt-action .410 with hands that were sweating as much from anticipation as from the unseasonable heat. He alternately crept and crawled toward the distant piece of umber stubble that held the mourning dove. All the while he rehearsed the safety let-off, gun mount, and swing-through that would fold up the flushing dove. Sensing that he had arrived at the right spot, he slowly rose to his feet. The surprised dove sprang up a dozen yards to his right. From their distant hiding place, the two other boys saw the almost simultaneous puffs of smoke and feathers before they heard the sharp crack of the .410 and Frank's triumphant yell.

The stalking sequence was repeated in round-robin fashion by the youthful hunting alliance until the doves stopped feeding. After the final shot was taken that late autumn afternoon, seven gray birds lay in a neat row on the rusted railroad track alongside the proud hunters. Not an enviable harvest, but one that time and abundance would never diminish. The boys talked guns and hunting for some time before the waning light sent them down the tracks for home and chores.

Companions since we were toddlers, Frank, David, and I had prepared for that dove foray for years. We wore out slingshots and BB guns together—plinking bottles, shooting hand-sailed Mason-jar lids, and, when we really felt cocksure of ourselves, knocking soda caps out of the air with our Daisys. When Frank was off his eye, David couldn't miss. When they both lost their touch, I would shine their eyes. Together we were always on target.

Growing up on poor coal-mine wages earned by fathers who were lost to us on the graveyard shift, we always had a wealth of things to do in the woods and waters on our side of the tracks. Shooting and hunting were a rural rite of passage—something well-heeled city folks infected with materialism could never really understand. Because of our country upbringing and the joy it gave us, we never felt underprivileged. We were richly rewarded every time we ventured afield for fun or game, oblivious to the unnatural clamor of a world drunk on progress, a world that would soon intoxicate each of us with dreams of fame and fortune that would take us far away from the country and each other.

The week before our first dove opener, Frank and Dave came over to my house to plan our strategy for the hunt. "Think your dad'll let us use the Stevens?" David asked in his typical soft-spoken manner.

"Don't know," I responded.

"When ya gonna ask him? Ain't no way we're gonna kill doves with our BB guns, that's for sure," Frank lamented, wringing his ball cap in his hands.

"If he doesn't have to work this weekend," I promised, "I'll ask him before he gets into the Sunday paper or starts fixin' something around the house."

"Without that gun, we're sunk," Frank sighed.

"And, even if we do get to use it," David said, "what are we going to use for shells?" During those times, opening a new box of shells was a ritual akin to tearing the wrapping paper off your main gift on Christmas morning. Even when our dads were working full time, money was as scarce as thirty-bird coveys, especially for nonessential items like shotshells.

We peered over the candy counter in Spontak's corner grocery store at the neatly stacked pyramids of three-inch .410 boxes and other Monarch game loads displayed for all the hunters in our small corner of the world to see. Old man Spontak had already sold last fall's supply of shells to squirrel hunters a month earlier. These were fresh shells, their gleaming boxes adorned with colorful images of winging waterfowl, flushing quail, and darting hares.

"What you boys want?" Mr. Spontak grumbled in Russian-tarnished English from behind his porcelain-and-glass meat cooler.

"How much for a box of .410 shells?" Frank worked up the courage to ask.

"One dollar sixty-five cents," he grunted over the hum of his meat slicer. "Does your papas say it's okay for you to buy?" he added. We looked at each other, pockets too empty to buy even a piece of penny candy, and began shuffling out of the store.

"We'll be back for a box later," Frank shouted bravely before the screen door slammed behind us.

"Yeah, sure! Yeah, sure!" the old storekeeper huffed, without lifting his head from his work. Mr. Spontak's brusque demeanor always made us feel like we were wasting his time even when we had money to spend.

As we trudged down the street to my house, David, always the optimist, tendered a scheme we all deplored but resorted to often when we needed to buy wheels and axles for our soapbox carts, handlebar streamers, new baseballs, and such. Painfully familiar with the routine, we crisscrossed the back alleys and byways of our neighborhood, rounding up every glass bottle that had a price on its head. Rummaging through fetid trash cans and smoldering garbage dumps left a lasting impression, if not a lingering stench, on each of us, placing a premium value on every slender shotshell we would shoot. After a mountain of bottles had been sorted through and deposited on Mr. Spontak's golden oak counter, he grudgingly opened his ancient cash register and rewarded us with enough change for candy and a crisp new box of .410s.

"You boys shoot careful," he cautioned, glaring at us over his gold-rimmed bifocals, "or I tell you papas!"

When the weekend arrived, I approached my dad carrying the Sunday paper and, in a voice oozing honor and obedience, asked him if I could use the bolt-action Stevens to hunt doves. "Sure, son," he said without hesitation, "and tell your two huntin' buddies to 'shoot careful' too." Frank and David were quietly waiting for the verdict on our back porch. When I danced by the back door and gave them the thumbs-up sign, their eyes lit up like mine. Their fenderless bikes kicked up dust trails as they rode off to butter up their dads for permission to hunt doves opening day.

Like the paper shells and old shotgun we carried into the sheep pasture on that first dove outing, much would change in the sporting world and in our lives before we would become full-fledged birdhunters. However, in spite of the ravages of time and the vagaries of fate, one element has remained unchanged since that exciting dove hunt many years ago: the thrill of the hunt still stalks my pursuit of gamebirds.

Youngest of that country-bred trio, I have spent every September since that first season in dove-infested fields. Over the years, my armament has increased in stature along with my waist size. The Winchester Model 21 I take afield now completes the picture I imagined as a boy of what a grown-up dove hunter should carry into each new season. My ratio of shells expended per dove bagged has also improved some, but not enough to swell my ego or brag about to my friends. What I lacked in gun quality and gunning technique as a youngster, I more than made up for with untarnished reflexes, keen eyesight, and sheer determination.

These days dove hunting requires careful planning and much deeper pockets, or at least it seems that way. A properly cultivated and bush-hogged sunflower field doesn't come cheap, especially for such a comparatively short season. Neither does the time spent away from career and hearth. However, some state fish and game departments are making the sporting life more accessible for dove hunters of meager means. State-cultivated and managed public hunting areas, prudently administered, can rival the finest private clubs for dove-shooting opportunities. Whether on public domain or private ground, sunflower seeds attract doves like no sheep pasture ever could. Opening day in one of these carefully manicured fields can be an incredible shooting experience. Shooters quickly develop swivel necks and preferred shot selections as the birds bore in from every conceivable direction. Waves of darting and diving targets demand quick reaction and perfect timing. Misses during such a fusillade are soon forgotten. Shot and shell expenditure is ultimately measured in lost volleys and empty ammo boxes. When I'm on, a .410 Superposed can be a delight. When the "miss Medusa" raises her ugly head, a 12-bore shellshucker can seem pitifully inadequate. Either way, a day spent in the sunflowers is often as fleeting as the evening flight and as lasting as a double on doves.

I have always considered dove shooting as a warm-up for the upcoming waterfowl and bird seasons. To retrain dormant musculature and desk-bound reflexes, I usually lug out my ponderous old 12-gauge autoloader along with case lots of 2¾-dram, 1-ounce loads in Number 8 shot—a far cry from the skimpy patterns thrown by the old .410 Stevens. Once I get the long-barreled blunderbuss tracking, it helps compensate for my natural inclination early in the season to abbreviate my follow-through. As my graying hair thins and the flab encroaches, I need all the help I can get. I can remember a rare day in September, some years back, when I was the first to quit the field with a limit of doves, a hot little 28-gauge double gun cracked open over my shoulder. My two hunting buddies each gave me the thumbs-up as I passed them on my way out of the field. Such rare days are the stuff hope is made of. Considering my wingshooting performances of late, I truly hope my memory of such days serves me well into my golden years.

When late August starts to dry out the summer's heat and its lazy evenings begin cooling the grain fields, I often recall my first dove hunt in a distant, windblown pasture. My companions that shining day have both limited out, one succumbing to war wounds, the other to a cancerous nightmare. But in a sense they are still there with me every time I hunt the gray ghosts of autumn—taunting me when I miss, helping me discern distant incoming doves from departing dragonflies, delivering me from an old man's delusion of ever mastering the art and science of taking birds on the wing. Ever since that first time, the opening day of dove season has ushered in a flood of fond memories of seasons filled with hurried wingbeats, pungent gunsmoke, panting bird dogs, and amber game fields. To ever miss opening day would be an affront to those no longer in the field and an admission that the hope of another season will be reduced to nothing more than a fading recollection. That's why every September, Lord willing, you will find me ghosting the edges of a shimmering dove field, hoping for just one more chance to redeem myself, especially in the eyes of two old hunting buddies who have already quit the field.

Graven Images

"Pretty is as pretty does," Uncle John announced as I lifted the elaborately engraved L. C. Smith to my shoulder. Filled with July heat and hordes of people, the antique building was the hot attraction at the county fair that summer. Jostled by the large crowd and hampered by poor lighting, I had a difficult time inspecting the workmanship on the old Monogram Grade Smith. Although the wood-to-metal and metal-to-metal fit was superb, it was the engraving that held me trance-like.

"Just remember, all that chicken scratchin' won't add any more sparkle to your shootin' eye," Uncle John admonished, as I sized up the antique dealer for a frontal attack.

The portly dealer wasn't gunwise, but he was savvy enough to notice that I had more than a passing interest in the side-by-side. We dickered and fenced for twenty minutes or so, coolly fighting back the sweat brought on by the heat of battle. I won—sort of. As usual, Uncle John was right. The handsome Smith wasn't the bird-killing panacea I had hoped for, but it did prime my appreciation for the engraver's art.

My first outing with the glamorous Smith confirmed Uncle John's unsolicited words of wisdom. It was the quail opener, and we had no sooner released Uncle John's brace of dogs when they skidded to a point alongside a weedy fencerow thirty yards from the truck. I hastily slipped a pair of low-brass Number 8s into the 12-gauge Smith and motioned to Uncle John that I would take the far side of the fenceline. His sinewy English pointers were rock-solid as I clodhopped down a furrow opposite the dogs while watching Uncle John stump-leg-it into shooting position. The birds were moving—the dogs told us—they alternately pussyfooted and pointed, their heads vaning and their nostrils testing the steady southeast wind that carried the bird scent.

Up they came! Two dozen wild chances, clawing for air, scattered in the wind. Uncle John bounced one into the corn stubble on his side of the fence before I could separate a target from the exploding mass. A hen bird peeled off the covey and darted to my left. My right barrel couldn't catch up to her. A buzzing cockbird shot straight down my side of the fencerow. My left barrel didn't know right from wrong, either, for the plump bird sailed off unscathed.

"Nice shootin'," Uncle John shouted as I lowered the pretty Smith from my shoulder. He raised a pair of freshly killed birds and said, "Here's what we're after, boy!"

Dejectedly, I reloaded, took a step, and a single flushed behind me. As it angled across the plowed field, I wheeled and fired. Twice. For all I know, that cagey quail is still snickering to its roost mates. Uncle John raised the birds once again, but, seeing the scowl on my reddening face, refrained from commenting on my dismal performance.

"Sure is a pretty gun you got there," he said as we headed down the fencerow. "Let's see if we can find it some more birds."

The brushy fenceline led us to a cattle-trodden field of fescue that couldn't hide an undernourished shrew. Just as the pointers started acting birdy, a single flushed a short step in front of me and flew straight away. I glided the elegant Smith to my shoulder, touched the front trigger, yanked the back trigger, then watched Uncle John suspend the bird in a cloud of feathers. I was speechless.

"The beauty of that gun must be blindin' ya, boy," Uncle John quipped as he reached down to take the bird from his dog.

"Yeah," I responded, "I'd like to see you do any better with this old cannon."

"Hand me that comely wench," he replied without hesitation. "Let me see what I can do with 'er."

We traded guns and cast the dogs toward a small stock pond surrounded by head-high cedars and thigh-deep broomstraw. In pursuit of the spirited dogs, I circled right and Uncle John headed left of the pond. When the dogs tightened the noose at the other end, they stopped almost in unison, facing each other on point. When we arrived on the scene, the birds immediately flushed in a ball and fled back over our heads toward the pond. Uncle John pivoted and fired once, twice. Two stone-dead bobwhites splashed the pond simultaneously with the pointers. I finally grounded a late-flusher with Uncle John's bobbed-barrel Model 11 Remington. As we watched his pointers clamber up the muddy bank with the quail, Uncle John said casually, "You know, I could get used to a gun like this." Before I could tell him he was shooting way above his class, his dogs, now shaking

Herb Booth

in unison, showered me with dirty pond water and mud. And so it went for the rest of that bird-filled hunt. Uncle John took his limit with as many shells, the lovely old Smith answering everything he asked of it.

My next trip with the Monogram was to the gravel pit behind our clubhouse. David propelled clay birds with a hand trap while I fired round after round without dusting a target.

"Boy, that sure is a beautiful piece of wood and steel," David remarked.

"Don't start." I recoiled. "If I never hit another living thing, you and Uncle John are not going to talk me out of this gun."

Like frantic wingbeats, the seasons sped past all too swiftly, and my futile attempts to tame the Smith took many turns. Its compelling beauty led me down the long, winding road to slip-on recoil pads, layered moleskin on the comb, hand protector on the barrels, ivory front and center beads, and hand-loaded shells— all to no avail. The wonderfully engraved Smith insulted and embarrassed me every time I hunted the gun, alone or with my companions. "Elsie" was no lady to me. But just one glance into the limpid swirls gracing its delicate lockplates and I would return for more abuse, ashamed for ever doubting its bird-killing pulchritude. I swooned over the shapely Smith for many bird seasons, never really understanding its mysterious power over me, never mastering its fickle moods. Engraving can have that affect on a gun lover.

An ancient art form, engraving has embellished fine objects for thousands of years. From gilt-edged swords and body armor to banknote printing plates and lead crystal, engravers have used numerous mediums to express their art form. Past masters like Rembrandt and Whistler brought hand-engraving to its pinnacle during the Renaissance. Firearms, especially, provide an excellent medium for the engraver's art. Many of England's best double shotguns and rifles reflect museum-quality engraving, as do most of America's older high-grade side-by-sides. And though I must admit that fancy engraving adds nothing to the function of a fine shotgun, it can certainly enhance pride in ownership.

Like everything else in the traditional gun trade, engraving requires a long and tedious apprenticeship. Young engravers are set to the task of engraving pins (screwheads), practicing on brass, and other menial undertakings before they are allowed to apply their hand gravers to gunmetal. Basically, three types of old-world engraving are still in existence: the classic English rose and scroll style (which was executed particularly well on my Monogram Smith), the Germanic deep-relief motif, and the Italian banknote *(bulino)* style. Interestingly enough, some of the most intricate and compelling works of art are accomplished with very simple tools such as hand gravers, hammers, and chisels, etc. It is exacting work that must be done confidently and precisely. Mistakes in gun steel, like broken promises to the fairer sex, are not easily erased.

In the gunmaking process, once the action filers have completed their burnishing strokes on the frame, trigger-guard bow, and fore-end furniture, the action, and the smoothly struck barrels are delivered to the engraver "in the white." Depending on the pattern and number of precious-metal inlays (gold, silver, platinum), an English best-grade double can consume weeks of the master engraver's time before the gun is ready for final finishing.

During the golden age of the English gun trade (1890-1930), even the more elaborate patterns became routine for the accomplished engravers of that period. World War II all but sealed the fate of the traditional gun trade in England, Europe, and elsewhere.

However, custom engraving will always command respect and princely sums from those of us who demand the finest in double guns. Whenever I am in the presence of an attractively engraved shotgun, I am reminded of a hot summer day many years ago. I can still see Uncle John shaking his head incredulously as I slipped an old L. C. Smith into its tattered canvas-and-leather case.

"If you think all that artistic tinkerin's going to put more birds in the bag," he warned, "you're sadly mistaken, boy."

Every fall thereafter, Uncle John, through one transparent scheme or another, managed to borrow the old double for the entire bird season. Obviously, that fancy engraving didn't impress him a bit. However, he was deadly with the vintage double. For all its compelling beauty, I still can't hit a living thing with the gun. I suppose I have Uncle John to thank for that.

Driven Birds

Tension mounts with the staccato bursts of distant gunfire down the line that announce the arrival of fast-flying birds. Hands eager with anticipation clutch double guns whose names have been spoken by serious shotgunners for generations. Churchill, Boss, Purdey, and others, all hallmarks of a proud tradition in gunmaking excellence, stand in readiness. Behind each butt, man and gun rise to meet the waves of driven birds in wild flight across the heathered highlands. High overheads, low incomers, crossing rights—the birds test gun and shooter alike with a mixed bag of challenging shots. After the shoot, the top gun can reflect on the fast action and thank the good Lord and the gamekeeper for such spirited birds. He and the other shooters can also give thanks to England's talented gunmakers who have distilled form and function into its purest state—the English "best" game gun.

For well over a century, England has reigned supreme as the standard-bearer of state-of-the-art game guns. The shotgun world continues to imitate designs and production techniques perfected decades ago in the British Isles. And once discriminating shotgunners have sampled the rest of what the world has to offer, they invariably settle on an English best gun, or a reasonable copy, for their target and game shooting. Although the classic English double gun may never fall from grace, unfavorable economic climates and shooting trends have forced even some of the more renowned British gunmakers to cut production, while many others have been forced to close their doors. Such closures are a sad loss not only to England's colorful gunmaking heritage, including the London and Birmingham trades that nurtured it, but also to the shotgun fraternity the world over.

What goes around comes around. Many Old World game guns that once helped celebrate the pomp and pageantry of the English shooting field are finding new homes in the New World. And while Spanish *la perdiz roja* (red-legged partridge), Scottish red grouse, and English pheasants will lead multitudes of Anglos afield on the "Glorious Twelfth," American wingshooters are adapting stick-straight driven-bird guns to walk-up hunting for September grouse, October woodcock, and November quail.

With each passing season, America's love affair with the classic game gun reaches deeper into the heartland. In typical American fashion, these English doubles will be extensively tested—from the sharptail-grouse bluffs of Manitoba, across the fertile U. S. uplands, and into the whitewing-dove wintering grounds of Mexico. The temper of wood and steel is challenged by temperate climates that can strip case colors from poorly hardened receivers and denude stocks not treated to a proper London oil finish. American birdhunters are discovering that English game guns are built to take all the testing the continent has to give, and will continue to serve their masters for generations, given considerate care.

Though known more for innovative revolvers, pistols, and lever-action rifles, Americans, too, have a rich shotgunning history. Just before the twentieth century was ushered in, U. S. gunmakers with familiar names like Parker, L. C. Smith, and Dan Lefever employed Old-World artisans to machine-make and hand-fit side-by-sides that have created New-World reputations of their own. Progressive turn-of-the-century sportsmen could even order these well-made shotguns with scaled-down frames, streamlined barrels, and straight-hand stocks for light and lively field work. Some of these light-weight Parkers, Smiths, and Foxes are still giving good account of themselves in American coverts. In the higher grades, these discontinued double guns are commanding some impressive sums from collectors and birdhunters alike.

However, and just as I did for years, many nostalgic gunners are needlessly handicapping themselves with tightly choked, long-barreled Yankee doubles that do not fit the shooting conditions or the shooter. The "heads-up" shooting style that was popular during America's double-gun Golden Age has bequeathed a legacy of crooked buttstocks that are at best uncomfortable to shoot. Through some painful experimentation, I eventually learned that a game gun custom-built to personal dimensions and desired quarry will measurably improve shooting consistency and comfort afield.

With the emphasis today being placed, as it should, more on quality gunning experiences than on the quantity of birds brought to bag, a double-gun renaissance of sorts is taking place across America. Aside from the welcome resurrection of the old Fox double gun (in very limited production), at present there exists no established gunmaker in the United States capable or willing to produce side-by-sides in the best-game-gun tradition. Every now and then, however, imitations of classic American and English doubles surface to briefly ride the uncertain waves of double-gun resurgence.

If you were to visit what remains of the old gun trade in England today, you would be transported back to an age when quality of craftsmanship and pursuit of perfection, not just profit, were the primary motives for building sporting arms. Reputations during Britain's gunmaking Golden Age were won or lost on the strength or weakness of an action. Throughout the ancient, cluttered shops, you would witness Old-World sentiment retained with a century-old leg vise and engraver's pitch still being used by a world-class engraver, or hand-hewn wood chisels scattered about a stockmaker's dusty bench, or an action filer's ever-present lampblack smudge pot used to joint doubles within a "thickness of smoke." There is something both humbling and intriguing about watching master gunmakers pursue their craft. Laboring tediously at the bench for hours on end to meet protracted production deadlines, each artisan strives to satisfy the pride and perfection that set traditional English doubles apart from the rest. Game guns built in the finest English tradition are a tribute to all who appreciate quality guns and meaningful shooting experiences.

Beginning with rough English nickel steel forgings and highly figured French walnut blanks, it takes a veritable symphony of skilled hands wielding files, chisels, gouges, and gravers to create masterpieces that will perform flawlessly for generations. A truly hand-built game gun in today's computer-automated world is an anachronism well worth its weight in gold.

If you are a connoisseur of smoothly struck, chopper-lump barrels, colorfully case-hardened action bodies, and precisely checkered walnut stocks, an English game gun will suit your demanding tastes rather nicely. And if driven birds are not your cup of tea, I suspect there will be more than a few American gamebirds bagged and shooters impressed by British game guns in the ensuing years. Considering the generations of utility built into these guns, they continue to redefine upland gunning standards.

The allure of a driven-bird shoot still flickers deeply within most ardent upland birdhunters, even if they are reluctant to admit it. The pomp and pageantry of the early turn-of-the-century English shooting parties often evokes images of a time when shooting flying birds was revered by royalty and rogue alike. Some American hunters consider a driven-bird shoot the height of arrogance, while others feel it is more shooting than hunting. Nonetheless it is an opportunity to refine wingshooting skills and revel in the rewards of nature's abundance and proper game management. Those who appreciate the privilege will enjoy the fast-paced shooting as well as the camaraderie of others whose appreciation for fine guns and fast-flying game is never completely sated. After a glorious day spent handling a matched pair of Stephen Grant Lightweights, James Purdey Special Engraved guns, John Dickson round actions, Holland & Holland Deluxes, or the like, it is understandable why driven birds still command the respect and admiration of upland gunners the world over. If the guns are worthy of the game, an enjoyable experience can be had by all.

I must admit, the closest I have ever come to an honest-to-goodness Edwardian driven-bird shoot was at Winchester's Nilo Farms, near East Alton, Illinois. I was the guest of some preeminent conservationists who were enjoying Winchester's hospitality in grand style. After a morning of following braces of energetic English springers through sprawling fields of well-manicured food plots brimming with pen-reared quail and chukar, we lunched on sumptuous pheasant pot pie and prepared for an afternoon mallard shoot. The shooting season was nearing its end, and it seemed this prestigious preserve had exhausted its supply of flighted mallards. Undaunted by the predicament, our hosts substituted pheasants for ducks to pacify the wingshooting desires of our shooting party. Standing in corn-stalked blinds (butts) scattered along a deep valley floor, we expended piles of Super-X shotshells on the pheasants that sailed high overhead. I tumbled a few, but to a birdhunter weaned on flushing quail, it was a humbling experience.

When I related the shoot to my hunting partners down home, I was brought back down to earth. Always the gunning analyst, David said that the pistol-gripped Winchester Model 23 double I shot probably had too much drop to consistently take the high-flying incoming birds. Frank candidly told me that "a dove is a duck is a pheasant when pass shooting. If you lead'm right," he proclaimed, "what's the damn gun got to do with it?" When Mark heard about the "driven pheasants," he just shook his head and said he didn't know how anyone could shoot a game bird that wasn't properly pointed by a good bird dog. "If you ask me," Luke lectured me, "you were standin' in pretty tall cotton with all those Nilo fellas and shootin' way over your small-town head to begin with."

Provincially minded as always, Luke was seldom impressed with my worldly adventures.

From mist-shrouded moors to heather-scented uplands, driven-bird shooting has left its mark on British game-gun form and function. The guns in turn are leaving their imprint on a new generation of shooting sportsmen an ocean removed from the Anglo-Saxon islands that spawned them. Birdhunters are fortunate indeed that tradition dies hard in Great Britain and that the red grouse and gaudy ringneck are still being driven to exact the best from game guns and game gunners on both sides of the Pond, small-town opinions notwithstanding.

Ahead
of the Game

A natural progression of events leads a country boy
from rock throwing, slingshooting, BB gunning,
and .22 plinking to grown-up shotgunning. Each
step instills an almost instinctive feel for how to
lead a target. You might call it a wingshooter's rite
of passage, often punctuated with liberal doses of
unsolicited advice from one's shooting elders.

Lead, or "forward allowance" as the British call
it, can be as difficult to explain as a woman's predilection for expensive French perfume. I have heard
old-timers lecture Nimrods about how they should
lead wind-darting doves by as much as a boxcar, and
swing through crossing bobwhites by a short beak or
a long neck. Wide-eyed and open-mouthed in youthful naivete, I listened intently to such palaver during
my formative years, but often wondered if these sages
of marsh and field were really trying to sharpen my
shooting eye or just bending my ear.

"Well, sonny," one would say, "just plant that ole
bead three feet in front of a skyrocketing grouse, slap
the trigger, and retrieve your bird."

"Now you can try it your own way, kid," another
would advise, "but take my word for it, you've got to
calculate your lead by dividing the speed of the bird

Herb Booth

by its distance from the muzzles, then add in wind direction, the bird's angle of departure, the constriction of your choke, length of the shot string . . . and, uh, don't forget to subtract your delayed reaction time caused by that hemlock branch waving in your face. When you can do it all in the twinkle of an eye, kid, you'll be a bird-killin' son of a gun!"

Sound familiar? Age and experience afield have since helped me distill such insightful instruction into a single word: bullfeathers!

Ask a gridiron-wise quarterback how much he leads a pass receiver, and if he's honest, he won't be able to tell you. The same holds true for shooting. Everyone's mental and physical computer is unique. The programmed split-second adjustments for "forward allowance" are entirely personal. Constant practice makes them almost second nature, if not "instinctive." There is no substitute for field experience, especially if you're equipped with a shotgun that fits. Practice also builds confidence, perhaps the single most important element for consistent shooting.

During World War II, the U. S. armed forces trained antiaircraft gunners on the skeet range. With shotgun in hand, each gunner learned how to swing through targets, further ingraining the elusive concept of lead in their minds in preparation for bigger game.

More often than not, I'll miss a bird because I didn't swing through the target after yanking the trigger. This same nemesis can visit golfers, bowlers, tennis players, and other sporting folks who must learn to coordinate hand and eye into one fluid motion. Any interruption of "forward allowance" brought about by fatigue, cumbersome clothing, or dense foliage will make hunters frown and ammo makers smile. Within twenty-five yards, a normal bird load's velocity and short shot string will require less "forward allowance" but more precise pointing. At longer ranges, a greater lead coefficient must be programmed in to help compensate for shot spread and bird speed. A stint at the patterning board and realistic clay-target practice will add up to more hits in the field.

All logic aside, if you really want to know how to lead a bird without referring to a barn full of ballistics, find some snooker-shootin' old-timer whose feats with a smoothbore are well known, if not self-professed, and stay well out of earshot of the old reprobate. Just watch. Both you and your shooting will improve commensurately.

By the way, when I was in college, "forward allowance" had an entirely different meaning. But don't take my word for it—just ask my old man.

Just One More Gun

The covey thundered up just beyond my dog's picturesque point, quickly dispersing through the thick oak woods that bordered the picked cornfield. My Parker came up for the third time in a double-barreled attempt to down a bird for my dog and the game bag. Like my own thundering volleys in the woods that crisp fall morning, those three covey flushes echo vividly in my memory. I suppose I am fortunate to have understanding hunting partners, a forgiving dog, and a resilient ego. But missing those "give-me" shots with both barrels three times in one day still plagues me.

Perhaps it was the conservation banquet the night before that dulled my middle-aged reflexes. Or maybe it was the new recoil pad my friend Luke convinced me to slip over "Old Reliable's" skeleton butt to give it the extra length of pull he was sure I needed. If my shooting had been as polished as my excuses, I would have had my limit of birds on that unforgettable opening day. Blaming the gun, of course, would have further insulted my hard-won reputation as a passable wingshooter and shotgun authority, if not set me off on another futile crusade for the "perfect" bird gun.

Fortunately, three decades of birdhunting have taught me that every sojourn afield is a new adventure, a new opportunity to exalt or demean my shooting prowess. In the end, I suppose, the birdhunter's ultimate rewards are watching the dogs work, enjoying the companionship of a good hunting partner, experiencing the rush of a covey flush. Come to think of it, deep-fried quail are not all that bad either, especially with a side helping of dirty rice and a carafe of palate-cleansing dinner wine. Then again, a trusty bird gun to rub on at day's end helps seal in birdhunting memories for a lifetime.

As a result of my lifelong quest for upland birds and classic double guns, my den has become a shrine of sorts. Books, bronzes, and art prints sag its bookshelves and festoon its walls, further magnifying the mystique and deepening my reverence for the sporting way of life. I am a hopeless captive of its yearlong enchantment. Bird dogs, being what they are, consume most of my conscious thoughts before, during, and after bird season. Not surprisingly, bird guns take up what's left. Such a preoccupation is not exactly a formula for marital bliss, but it certainly can be a prescription for a long and rewarding life.

Just when I think I have distilled birdhunting down to a one-gun affair—a shapely smoothbore that fits my physique and my fancy—one of the boys introduces me to a new "gotta have" upland wonder gun. My nemesis this season is a sweet little 28-gauge side-by-side of foreign persuasion. It's a no-name boxlock made in Liege, Belgium, no doubt a "lunchbox" gun carried home piece by piece by a bone-weary slave of the old gun trade. Lost amid a forest of paramilitary firearms, the 28 leaped off the table at a gun show and followed me home. Thank God providence was smiling on me in the form of an IRS refund that needed recycling. This, coupled with a spare gun case I happened to have tucked away in the trunk of my car, helped me smuggle the little beauty home without arousing my wife's suspicions or gutting our joint checking account. It's not that I'm afraid to assert my male dominance as lord and master of the household; I have simply learned the hard way that where long-suffering wives and new guns are concerned, discretion dictates prudent tactics. Believe it or not, ignorance under such circumstances helps preserve marital bliss. And should the ruse be discovered by my trusting spouse, I won't hesitate to plead the Second Amendment.

With any new addition to the gun cabinet, there is usually a bittersweet period of adjustment between hunter and gun. After my initial blush of "new gun" romance faded some and my subconscious began registering a few twinges of buyer's remorse, closer scrutiny of the piece revealed some imperfections. There were a few things the poor gun-show lighting had failed to illuminate and my impassioned eye had failed to recognize. The Greener-type crossbolt did not always return flush to the fence when the little darling was closed—a simple adjustment, no doubt. Using snap caps, I dry-fired the gun several times, alternating the trigger sequence and testing trigger pulls. Four pounds on the front, three-and-a-half on the back. All in all, not too bad. The selective ejectors even kicked the heavy snap caps a good distance and reasonably close together. They seemed well regulated and well timed. Somewhat disturbing, though, was the wood creep I felt on the fore-end whenever the gun was cocked. This too, was probably a minor adjustment any experienced gunsmith could make.

Overall, the bores were bright, the case-hardening was a well-aged blend of rainbow colors, and the borderline engraving looked as if it had been done with a hammer, chisel, and hand graver. The checkering was tight, clean, and about twenty-two lines to the inch. The 28-inch barrels were virtually ripple free, and the swamped rib didn't show any signs of shedding solder or flux. Metal-to-metal and wood-to-metal fit appeared to be hand wrought within a wisp of smoke.

After a few days of stroking and fondling the nimble 28 bore and parading it around my comrades at the gathering place, my passion for the pre-World War II gun was at a fever's pitch. David, with the rest of the boys nodding their approval, gave me an unsolicited sermon on the folly of forsaking my American shotgun heritage for some twin-tubed Mata Hari. Inspired though it was, it failed to dampen my ardor for the gun. To increase its length of pull, I added a leather slip-on pad to the straight-hand stock and dry-fired the gun at spots on my den walls for a few weeks before arranging an informal round of hand trap at the pit behind the gathering place. Everyone was anxious to see me smoke some clays with the "prissy" little gun.

Although duly cautioned by David, I neglected to have my Belgian affectation thoroughly gone over by an expert gunsmith (more scarce these days than honest politicians). Superficial attraction can be very deceiving, if not fatal, especially when courting a vintage double of dubious origin. But since this trimly built little beauty was destined to be my upland soulmate for life, I never questioned the gun's genealogy or integrity.

When that bright autumn day dawned over our back-forty shooting ground, I strutted a little as I called for the first clay target. Bristling with self-confidence and great expectations, I instructed my shooting companions to take special note of how a properly made, well-fitted, small-bore game gun could smoke clay birds. With supreme confidence I yelled, "Pull!" The speeding target played directly to my port-side gun mount and follow through. I was dead sure of the shot. When I fired, the discharging side-by-side jerked well above the target path, and it took me several moments to realize I was holding a two-piece gun. Upon firing, the dainty, horn-tipped fore-end parted company with the wispy barrels and frame. I was devastated but unharmed. Tears of unrequited love were beginning to well up in my disbelieving eyes when I heard Frank wryly announce, "You sure smoked that one!"

The next day I rushed over to visit my friendly Smitty. "Where've you been, boy?" he asked, his eyes embracing the dainty double as I slipped it from the case. "Get this over at the gun show, did ya?" he smirked as I handed him the gun. "Wish I could've gone with you—could've saved you some money."

He broke down the gun, inspected it briefly, and said the Anson-type push-rod spring had lost its temper (ain't it just like a lady?), allowing the fore-end to come loose on recoil. He quickly replaced the spring and augured in a couple of fore-end screws to prevent any further wood creep upon cocking.

My amorous feelings for the foreign temptress were beginning to buoy once again when Smitty casually announced that the barrels were slightly off the face of the action. He held the standing breech

up to his lamp, and I grimaced as a sliver of light sliced through the gun. My knees buckled and my stomach sank at this unexpected revelation. Before breaking out into a cold sweat in front of my irascible old friend, I took a deep breath and inwardly questioned my powers of judgment, my suitability as a spouse, and my maternal parentage.

A small king's ransom later, I finally had a double gun that was safe to shoot. I have even managed to give a good account of myself on subsequent trips to the back-forty shooting grounds. The double-barreled coquette has also downed a number of pen-raised birds for my dog. But like a woman scorned, I have never really felt completely comfortable or confident with the slimly built side-by-side ever since that first shot. The attractive little double gun does fill a long-overlooked niche in my upland battery, but if I had just one more gun, perhaps a Stephen Grant lightweight or a Charles Lancaster "12-20," I would at last own the ultimate bird gun. With such a gun I would never again be distracted from fiscal responsibility or domestic duty. Just one more gun. Considering the high cost of true love these days, is that really too much to ask?

Stock and Trade

It was early spring and while other high school juniors were polishing cars, strutting in tuxes and buying corsages for the big prom, I was busy whittling on a replacement stock for an old Fox Sterlingworth double. By the time the cute, teenage girl across the street worked up enough courage to ask me to the dance, I had managed to sever a tendon in my thumb with a dull wood chisel, bludgeoning an otherwise beautiful piece of American black walnut in the process. Had the buttstock not been 90 percent inletted by the manufacturer, I probably would have lost the use of both hands before successfully mating wood to metal. Considering the way I danced at the junior prom, I should have dropped the chisel on my foot. I came away from the entire experience with a much greater appreciation of the stockmaker's craft, female forbearance, and the Tennessee Waltz.

In the English gun trade, an apprentice will spend many years under the tutelage of a master stocker before he is allowed to ply his talents on a "best" gun. During that time, he will learn how to translate a customer's try-gun dimensions into a gunstock that fits. He will also grade and study the grain of English, French, and Circassian walnut. He won't begin shaping the wood until it has been properly dried and retains a moisture content of between 6 and 12 percent. He will use an assortment of hand tools that would intimidate a pit-crew mechanic. And, because many of these tools are so specialized, he must first learn how to fabricate them from raw wood and cold steel.

The epitome of shotgun craftsmanship, a best grade English sidelock double takes months to inlet, checker and finish. To accommodate the gun's intricate lockwork, the stocker smokes the metal parts with lamp black, presses them against the wood and cuts away the blackened contact points until the lockwork is firmly housed within the jaws of the stock. Because of their mechanical makeup, boxlock doubles require less (but no less precise) inletting. As sophisticated as modern technology can be, there is still no machine on earth that can duplicate the subtle wood-to-metal fit achieved by the master craftsman's knowing hand and keen eyes. A stock fitted and finished in the best English tradition is as much a work of art as it is a functional unit for shouldering the gun. Such laborious attention to detail is but one of the many reasons a best-grade double gun can take from six months to three years to be delivered, and cost a small fortune.

More often than not, the stock of a best grade double will exhibit a chaste amount of fine-line checkering (usually 24 to 32 lines per inch) and a London oil finish. If the walnut is densely grained and properly aged, it will be turned into powder by the razor-sharp checkering tools. Whenever I ring up master stocker David Trevallion, I can always tell when he is checkering by the telltale puffing sound he makes to clear his working surface of the wood dust. Once a master stockmaker at Purdeys in London, Trevallion emigrated to the United States and is now stocking and gunsmithing out of his own shop in Maine. On more than one occasion he has told me that the traditional gun trade suffers from too much rock 'n' roll and not enough teenagers willing to undergo the demanding apprenticeship that custom stockmaking requires. David apparently had the same adolescent experience I had on the dance floor, but managed to stick to his guns.

To a stock fancier, there is probably no prettier sight on god's green earth than the glowing beauty of a London oil finish. Applied by hand day after day, week after week, the finish is rubbed deep into the wood. During the heyday of the gun trade, many oil formulas were passed from father to son and became closely guarded secrets. Most of these recipes included linseed oil, wax polish and some other form of hardener to accelerate drying. Properly applied, an oil finish protects and beautifies the wood, highlighting and sealing the grain.

Next time you balk at the price of a Purdey, Boss, Parker A-1 Special, Winchester Model 21 Grand American, or any other high-grade shotgun, remember the simple rule of "thumb" I learned to live by early in life: Don't try to chisel your way out of paying the piper if you want to dance with a pretty lady.

The Gathering Place

Once, there were good friends to greet, wild game to hunt, and time to kill. The world was a slower place. Hunting was part of the natural scheme of things. Few of us saw the change coming. Like the passing of the seasons, it was unstoppable, inevitable.

The headlong rush for material wealth had condemned the gathering place. Overrun by civilization, the timbered edifice sagged and groaned from neglect, a forgotten relic destined for the developer's dozer. Along with woodsmoke from the tired building's chimney, old men's yarnspins and boyhood dreams had long since drifted off into the heavens.

Silver-haired and timeworn, I had returned once again to the gathering place to hear the human heart pour out its love for the alluring woods and enchanted marsh, to rekindle old friendships, old memories. The familiar chairs, in a loose semicircle around the potbellied stove, were dust-laden, empty. I inspected the vent and tested the draft on the rusted old stove and rummaged in the cobwebbed kindling box for bits of fatwood to stoke up the fire that still burned deep within me. My worldly travels mostly complete, the gathering place was the only spot I never really wanted to leave.

The rickety pressed-back chair creaked loudly as I took my place in the gathering once again. Rheumy-eyed, I surveyed the seating places of my five missing comrades in arms. An empty cigar box protruded from under Uncle John's bentwood rocker. A proud campaigner of marsh and field, he ended his lifelong hunt in a suburban nursing home upstate. Frank survived the Asian war for a few seasons, eventually succumbing to his lingering wounds, his captain's chair patiently awaiting new orders. David, a crack shot with a shotgun, lost his battle with cancer—the polished caning in his spindled-oak chair was still sagging, still grieving. Young Mark, dog handler supreme, fell asleep at the wheel one late summer's eve on a long drive home, never to wake up. I can still see him perched on the edge of his beat-up orange crate, hanging on to every word uttered by his elders. And then there was brother Luke, who, with the assistance of a jealous husband, exchanged his life for a bottle of whiskey and a lonely wife. His cigarette-scarred bar stool stood a silent vigil, longing to be swiveled again among the gathering.

Settling down in the chair, I recalled the time Uncle John regaled the gathering with the hunting escapades of his city-bred nephew. Seems the youngster was acting pretty smug about his gun handling and persuaded Uncle John to invite him down for a quail hunt. Uncle John wasn't sure if the brash kid knew a bobwhite from a guinea hen, but felt compelled to oblige his kin.

Rocking rhythmically with the slow crackle of the fire, Uncle John began relating his story. "Well, we hit the broomstraw real hard that warm opening day," he said with a snicker, half puffing, half chewing on his cigar. "What my young nephew lacked in field knowhow, he made up for with his mouth. He went on and on all morning long about how he was going to shoot a quail feast for his buddies back in the big city. I offered advice on the finer points of birdhunting, but he wasn't hearing it.

"Lord, it was hot! My eager pointers were tripping over their tongues, and we still hadn't busted a covey. After lunch I retired the dogs and we split up to work the cover around Black Pond. There was always a covey or two holed up in the slashes along the east side of the pond. Before going our separate ways, I told my insolent nephew the birds might still be out in the weed fields bordering the heavy cover. I quickly covered the west side of the water without ruffling a feather. My stumpy legs and arthritic knee told me to take the shorter route.

"While catnapping against a deadfall, I heard no less than eighteen shots thunder across the pond. I began to wonder if the boy would run out of shells before he ran out of determination. I never moved that many birds on that side and began to cuss myself for taking the short way around the pond.

"Eventually, I heard brush crunchin'. There stood my blooded relative grinnin' like an old lady with a new hat. 'Sounds like you got into 'em real good,' I said. He reached into his game bag and smugly piled up eight of the plumpest birds you ever saw. I was amazed and amused by his identification ability. Without saying a word, I field-dressed his birds.

"My proud nephew, strutting like a bantam rooster, began crowing about how easily and skillfully he'd bagged his limit. I patted him on the back and sent him back to the city that evening with final cleaning instructions and a few choice recipes.

"Strange as it seems, he hasn't spoken to me since. To this day I'm dying to know how he and his urban buddies enjoyed their feast of dirty rice and Black Pond meadowlarks!"

The orphaned stove was ravenous. I fed it all the scraps of pine, oak, and hickory I could find until its fat belly glowed pink against the rafters.

Tall and taciturn, Frank was the first to buy his duck stamp each season. His stories, usually brief as the morning flight, were always spiced with sarcasm. Waterfowling ran thick in his blood.

One January morning we were gathered around the stove, weathering a shutter-rattling northwest

Herb Booth

wind, when Frank leaned back in his captain's chair and recounted an unforgettable adventure in the marsh. Looking each of us in the eye in turn, he began weaving his long-winded tale of woe.

"Took an old college roommate duck hunting once. Hadn't seen him in years. It was obvious he had more money than good sense. When I picked him up at the crossroads bus station that pitch-black morning, he looked more like the prey of a mail-order catalog than a duck hunter. Never saw so many gadgets and designer camo in my life.

"It was late in the season, with skim ice on the potholes, so I took him to a public hunting area out along the big river. He drank both thermoses of coffee before we were halfway there. Stopped three times to drain his enthusiasm. We had to claim our blind before 6 A.M. or risk losing it to other hunters. It was turning into one of those track-shoe mornings, and we were running out of time.

"The blind was a tough forty-five-minute trek from the parking area. I hoisted two bags of corkbodies and told my roomie to grab the guns and gear. Almost lost him twice in the dark. 'There any poisonous snakes in here?' he whined, sloshing slowly behind me. At least they had sense enough to get out of the cold. Looking back on it, I wish a fat old moccasin would've cut a wake in his direction that morning. Might've quickened his pace a little.

"Somehow we made it to the blind on time. He tripped on his way up the ladder, gashed his new waders on a nail, and soaked his woolies with ice-cold river water. He wailed like a turpentined cat. I fired up the heater to thaw him out and told him to sit still while I set the decoys. Well, the dumb s.o.b. started fooling around with the charcoal stove and caught the damn blind on fire. I wallowed back as quick by as I could and began pitching water on the flames with my hat. We were lucky. He only burned up half the blind. My half, as it turned out.

"Finally got settled in just as the sun peeked over the marsh to see what all the fuss was about. The wind picked up. Bundles of ducks began wheelin' around the backwater. It was a surefire mallard-killin' day. I quickly showed my roommate how to load his fancy new autoloader and asked him to hand me my pump gun. Yep, you guessed it. My beer-drinkin', woman-chasin' college roommate left it back at the car. There wasn't time to go back. Greenheads were already shining over the blocks.

"My partner was like a yo-yo in the blind. He spooked three bunches before I got him settled down. The birds were eager, though. Never touched my call. A lone drake hooked into the spread. Easy shot. I released my roommate's shoulder and told him to shoot. *Boom! Boom! Boom!* He raked the bird with his last shot. It hit the water, head up, in the middle of the decoys and began swimming away from the blind. 'Don't shoot until . . . *Boom!* . . . he gets out of the decoys!' I pleaded. Well, he blew the beak off one of my hand-painted corkbodies, killed his duck, and beamed like a kid at Christmas. Cussing uncontrollably, I retrieved the greenhead.

"When I returned to the blind, he was fiddling with his auto. 'Dumb gun's jammed,' he said, struggling to remove some part. *Poing!* He launched the magazine plug over the back of the blind. I searched in that tangle of marsh for nearly an hour. Couldn't find it. Meanwhile, the entire flyway of November mallards rained down our hole in the slough. Haven't seen a day like it since.

"The temperature kept dropping. My purple-lipped companion was shivering in his boots. I finally got the plugless gun back together, which was a signal for the birds to stop flying. They did. Enough was enough. My roommate had had it. I bundled him up with some of the gear, gave him my keys, and sent him back to the car. I kept his gun handy while I picked up the decoys. No luck. I called it quits.

"On my way out of the marsh, a conservation officer welcomed me back to the real world. Checked my license. Checked the gun. No plug. Gave him my best sob-story about the kind of morning I was having. No luck. He didn't buy a word of it. He wrote me up and sent me packing. It was a quiet drive home.

"That Christmas I got a letter from my old roomie telling me what a great adventure he had and that we must do it again soon. The letter laid around 'til well after duck season before I got around to answering it.

"Believe it or not, I still consider that duck hunt my most successful day in the marsh. After all, I lived to tell about it."

The bottomless potbellied stove, popping and creaking, cried out for more wood. I slowly began breaking up my companions' brittle wooden chairs, one by one, to keep the fire alive.

Mark was a great listener. Young and impressionable, he was an easy touch for the old-timers in the gathering place. He did, however, possess a quick wit and an understanding of bird dogs that belied his tender age. More than anything else, he wanted to be one of the men, to tell tall stories late into the night.

One evening in early November, after a limit-filled quail opener, everyone gathered around the stove to share highlights of the hunt. Mark cradled a bone-tired yearling setter that had earned an honored place in the gathering that day. It was a red dog, a field-bred Irish setter. The pup was about four months old and down on its luck when Mark rescued it from the county dog pound earlier in the year.

"He was in pitiful shape when I got him," Mark said, inching forward on his crate. "But he had a certain sparkle in his eyes that told me he was a born hunter. I brought the dog home and introduced him to my tricolor, who had the run of the place. Won't keep a dog unless I can make him part of the family. The pup wasn't faring too well, so I fasted him for a day before I wormed him. I watched him close, but I guess not close enough. Later that day, I ran to the store for some grub. When I got back, the pup's bowels had draped yards of ribbony white tapeworm all over the kitchen. It smelled for days. My house might look like a boar's nest, but my dogs more than make up for the mess come bird season.

"Lot of hunters keep their bird dogs in a kennel away from the house, away from the family. They feed 'em, give 'em their shots, and think they're taking care of all their needs. When bird season rolls around, they usually wind up hunting *for* their dogs, not with them. Like kids, bird dogs need lots of attention, especially setters. It's too late to make up for lost time when the leaves start fallin'.

"I always wanted a real Irish setter ever since I saw one on an ammo poster down at the hardware store. Sure are loyal dogs. I named this one Shadow. He follows me everywhere. The way I figure it, if you want your dog to perform, he's got to know as much about you as you do about him. Pedigree's nothin' if your dog don't trust you. Some of you said Shadow was a mind reader today because of the way he worked cover you thought held birds. I believe every good bird dog knows his master's mind as well as his own. If you have a bond with your dog, you won't have to whistle and holler yourself deaf to get him to hunt with you.

"I 'think' my dogs into a piece of cover. They read me like a book, and I share every page with them. Ever watch a pair of marsh hawks hunt? One sweeps low over the cover while the other stays in position to pounce on game. No different with a hunter and his dog. This pup's far from polished, but you saw how he kept checkin' back to see where I was. How he gave all the birds he retrieved to me. Dog trainers get results because they spend time with a dog. You have to develop the bond. Can't hurry it. Once a bird dog knows what you want, he'll break his heart to please you.

"Remember that cockbird you dropped in the farm pond, Dave? Shadow never hesitated. He plunged in to get that bird for me. And how about that brace you shot, Luke, in that honeysuckle thicket. The dog saw the birds fall and didn't give up until he found 'em both. But I was also in there, givin' him encouragement, thinkin' him through it. He's still got a way to go, but without the desire to please, all the learnin' and trainin' wouldn't mean a thing.

"How many of you would've given a plug nickel for an Irish setter before today?"

"Son," Uncle John interrupted, "if you ever took to preachin', you could convert the devil himself. I'll give you $500 for your red dog."

Herb Booth

"Really!" Mark replied, "Aw, but ya know I couldn't sell him."

"Thank God for that!" Uncle John chortled, rocking briskly in his chair. "Don't believe I could persuade the old ball-and-chain to set another place at the table."

"Oh, come on," Mark shot back, "give her more credit than that. It's never too late to teach an old dog new tricks!" Mark's long-awaited induction into the gathering place was seconded with laughter all around.

The wood from my companions' chairs had burned down to a bed of glowing coals. I opened the stove door and solemnly tossed in a large hand-polished, hand-carved pine knot. It bubbled and sputtered in the flickering embers before bursting into flame. The autographed knot was the final record of those who attended the gathering place.

Sensitive and soft-spoken, David was a true game-gun connoisseur. He also had an abiding reverence for the sporting life. Every so often someone would parade an old smoothbore around the gathering place. Without reading the barrel inscription or proof marks, David invariably identified it—name, rank, and serial number.

Late one fall evening, while we all recovered from a benefit feed put on by the women's auxiliary, David slid his newly caned chair back from the roaring stove and told the gathering about a one-of-a-kind bird gun.

"Got a call a few years back from a widow lady," he began. "Her late husband helped me out of a few financial jams during my upstart years. He was a big-time lawyer once, and why he settled in the country always puzzled me—that is, until the widow called. She said she was getting ready to sell a few of her husband's things. She remembered I was a hunter and didn't know anyone else who might want to buy her husband's hunting rifle. I never was that big on big game, but the woman sounded desperate over the phone, so a few days later I drove out to see her.

"If the widow's dilapidated Victorian house was any indication of her predicament, she was in real trouble. We exchanged pleasantries on the porch, sipped some fresh-brewed tea, and talked about the high cost of living. After a while, she led me up the stairs to her husband's study. The walnut-veneered room was hot and stuffy, and a few houseflies were loafing around the large leaded-glass picture window. Sporting books were stacked everywhere— rare autographed copies; leatherbound, gilt-edged books; slipcased first editions. She saw my interest and explained, 'When the Parkinson's set in, all he had left were his books. Lord knows what I'm going to do with them all.'

" 'Here's his rifle,' she said, pointing to a leather trunk case on his large executive desk. I unlatched the case and slowly raised the lid. 'Kind of gaudy, isn't it?' she sighed. My eyes swept over the graceful lines of the loveliest 20-bore side-by-side I had ever seen. Except for the faded green billiard cloth, the double looked as if it had just arrived from the factory, complete with snap caps and turn screws.

"I lifted the ivory- and horn-inlaid buttstock from the French-fitted case. The dark, oil-finished stock was finely carved and flawlessly checkered. It had more figure in it than a vaudeville chorus line. I inspected the scroll engraving on the sidelocks and marveled at the intricate gold-inlaid gamebirds. After carefully assembling the straight-hand gun, I snapped it to my shoulder. It responded as if made for me. It was an old Lefever, a rare Thousand-Dollar grade.

" 'Do you think I could get $300 for it?' she asked, breaking my reverie. I didn't know what to say. The grand old lady was struggling, I knew that. It was obvious her husband's illness had drained their life savings. Fighting back a rush of adrenaline, I told her I would check around to see if anyone might be interested. I also told her that if worse came to worst, I'd take the gun off her hands. She squeezed my hand in thanks, smiled with her trusting blue eyes, and bid me a safe journey home.

"I wrestled with my conscience for a few days, knowing full well I could make a killing off the gun. The temptation to take it and run was overwhelming. When I called her later that week, I gave her the phone number of a wealthy collector upstate. I also gave her the particulars on the Lefever and told her not to take a penny less than $30,000 for the gun. She was speechless. So was I.

"She called the next day to tell me the collector was on his way down with a cashier's check. She was sobbing over the phone. So was I, inside. I had just let a once-in-a-lifetime treasure slip through my fingers. That was the last conversation I had with the widow. Maybe, the windfall helped offset some of the tragedy of growing old without a spouse or an adequate income.

"Months later, a truck driver knocked at my door early one Saturday morning. Said he had a load of boxes for me and grunted loudly as he stacked them on my front porch. Before carrying them inside, I tore open a box. I was overcome with joy. The grand old lady had found a home for her husband's sporting library and a place in my heart forever."

The insatiable stove had consumed the last vestiges of my long-lost hunting companions. As much as I sensed their presence in the gathering place and felt the cares of the world retreating, I knew it would soon be time to go. I didn't know if I could pry myself from my chair one last time.

Brother Luke was the consummate "good ole boy"—wide grin, missing teeth, curly red hair, country through and through. Often earthy, seldom bashful, his backwoods philosophy was always on target.

Early one snowbound winter's eve, Luke took a slow pull on his ever-present jug and passed it around the gathering. Amid a chorus of raspy coughs and gasps, he swiveled around in his squeaky bar stool and told everyone about a kid brother who had forsaken his humble beginnings.

"Seems to me folks these days are rushin' off to everywhere and nowhere. Missin' out on what they already got. Take my baby brother, for instance. The whole family pitched in to put that boy through college. He's bright, all right. Books and writin' always came easy for him.

"When we were kids, he followed me around like a beagle chasin' a swamp rabbit. I taught him everything I could about the woods and huntin'. We were BB-gun terrors back then. Used to stack up spatsies and starlin's like cordwood. As usual, he was quick to learn. But he was a restless kid; you could see it in his eyes. Always jumpin' from one thing to another. There wasn't much he didn't know about huntin' by the time he went off to the university.

"Well, he did the family real proud. Graduated with honors. Education changed him, though. I didn't need no books to tell me what was written in his heart. The distant look in his eyes said he'd outgrown the country. He left home and landed a big-time job out on the East Coast. They sent him around the world chasin' the almighty buck. He always sent money home to mom, but didn't share much about what was goin' on in his life.

"Years shot past. He lost touch with the family and the land. Then one day outta' the blue, he calls and says he's comin' home for Thanksgivin'. Says he wants me to take him slug-huntin' for deer. Wants to know if grandpa's hammer gun's still in the closet. Wants a day or two alone in the woods. I told him to get his scrawny butt on an airplane and I'd have tags and guns waitin'.

"When I picked him up at the county airport, his eyes looked like two piss holes in a snowbank. I could see he was hurtin' real bad deep inside. Later on in the woods, he told me about a divorce and some big business deal that went sour.

"Next mornin' we were in the woods before dawn. Took him back of the mine ponds in the big timber along the Middle Fork creek bottoms. He didn't say much. Just took a deep breath every now and then. I could see it was goin' to take a while to brush the city dust off him. I set him against a lightnin'-struck stump beside an old deer trail. Told him to listen to the woods wake up, feel the wind in his face, watch the sunrise. He said I'd know if he got his deer. Told me to go on home without him if he didn't. I hunted in a big circle, hopin' to drive a buck past him. It seemed to get dark and cold all at once. Before leavin' the woods, I slipped quietly up the deer trail. Saw him leanin' against the stump, starin' off into the woods, a small fire flickerin' at his feet.

"He was still sittin' there the next mornin', woodsmoke hangin' over him like a halo. He looks up at me, his eyes burnin' red, and says, 'Big brother, God knows I've missed all this. Let's go get our deer.'

"Later that mornin' I heard grandpa's old Long Tom call once across the hardwood swamp. I came runnin'. Didn't know what I was goin' to find. When I came up on my brother, he was hunched over in a clearin', guttin' out the biggest damn ten-pointer you ever saw. We whooped and hollered like kids. He found what he'd lost.

"When we walked out of the woods that day, he had real fire in his eyes. He was alive inside. We

were brothers again. Still galls me some how lucky that kid is in the woods. I'll spend the rest of my days tryin' to top that buck.

"Now, no matter what, every Thanksgivin' me and my kid brother take to the woods. Long as I'm around, he's not goin' to miss out on another season. I've got to see to it that the fire keeps burnin' in his eyes. I don't ever want him rushin' off to nowhere again."

The fire was finally dead. The faithful old stove wept no more. The damp autumn chill returned once again to the darkened room. Bone-weary and spent, I slumped down in my lonely chair and accepted the cold. Time stood still in the gathering place. On the heels of my lost companions, fleeting images of slower times and golden days slipped silently through the chimney with the last wisp of smoke, wood-scented memories fading in the crisp night air.